A WARRIOR'S BATTLES

FOCUS ON THE FAMILY®

A WARRIOR'S BATTLES

MICHAEL ROSS
and Manfred Koehler

TYNDALE

Tyndale House Publishers, Inc.
Carol Stream, Illinois

To our *Breakaway* brothers:

*"If you do what is right, will you not be accepted?
But if you do not do what is right, sin is crouching at your door;
it desires to have you, but you must master it."*

—Genesis 4:7

CONTENTS

Week 4—Marks of a Battle-Ready Warrior

INTRODUCTION:

WAIT TRAINING THAT WORKS!

"God's Word to you is the same warning He gave to Cain (Genesis 4:7)—master the sin at the door of your life before it brings its inevitable and disastrous consequences. Heed His caution, and you will avoid unnecessary hardship for yourself and others." [1]—**Henry T. Blackaby**

Sixteen-year-old Alex of Tampa, Florida, feels defeated. "I'm a Christian," he told me, "but I get so caught up in the things of the flesh—especially lustful thoughts. I feel as if my faith has lost its fire, and I feel distant from God. What should I do?"

Now listen to the pain—and the hope—of a young man who asked to remain anonymous:

> Lust has been a battleground for me. I was first introduced to porn when I found some on my dad's computer. To be honest, I knew it was wrong, but I still looked at it. Then Satan began attacking my purity. But I serve a powerful God!

> We are called to flee from youthful lust (2 Timothy 2:22) and to intensely pursue righteousness! Psalm 119:9 asks the question, "How can a young man keep his way pure?" It says, "By living according to your word." The writer goes on and talks about seeking God with your whole heart. The way we can be pure is not by seeing how close we can get to the line without crossing it, but instead by seeing how close we can get to God.

> Each morning, I strive to make Hebrews 12:1-2 my prayer: "Lord, help me throw off the different sins that entangle me and allow me to run toward You with patient endurance."

Lust is a beast—a sharp-fanged, drooling monster that crouches at your door, waiting to poison your life with its self-centered craving. And I'm convinced that it's a teen guy's No. 1 battle. Some Christian boys even feel defeated, abandoned by God, and riddled with guilt for their weaknesses. Yet I've met others—countless others—who are winning the war. What's their secret? How are many teens able to stand strong, while others are giving up?

The answer is consistent *wait training*. Guys who are victorious have learned to face present and future temptations head-on. They've put into practice a purity game plan that works!

Read this book for 28 days straight and you, too, will learn how to master the sexual struggles that bombard your heart and mind. Here are some key training tips that you'll discover in the days ahead:

Tune in the truth. Too many boys listen to the lie Satan whispers in their ears. You know, the lie that "you're alone in this battle." You'll read dozens of stories from real teens who face the same struggles as you.

Purge any porn. We'll show you how to do the same with any other sexual material that causes you to fall.

Arm yourself with Scripture. God wants to renew your mind and shape your thinking about sex. You'll learn strategies for reading the Bible daily and discovering practical ways of applying Scripture to your life.

Build solid boundaries. Where are your weak areas? The Enemy attacks where guys are most vulnerable, and the easiest targets are the eyes and ears. You'll be challenged to steer clear of television programs, movies, music, Web sites, jokes, or friends who fuel warped messages about sex.

Find a training partner. All you need is a Christian buddy or two to share your commitment to purity. We'll show you what to do.

Consider the "father factor." You're at a stage in your life when you yearn for the affirmation and companionship of an adult male mentor (preferably your father). And when it comes to sexual struggles, fathers can offer wisdom, suggestions, and even more accountability. If your dad isn't in the picture, we'll give you tips for connecting with a trusted male relative, pastor, or youth leader.

Stand with a symbol. Get your hands on a purity cross, necklace, or ring that you can wear all the time to remind you of your commitment. Here's an idea: Go to www.breakawaymag.com and get a *TRIBE* wait training bracelet. It's an ideal companion to this book.

Don't worry, the training tips presented in *TRIBE: A Warrior's Battles* aren't reserved for holiest members of the Spiritually Elite Club. (That would completely exclude every guy who struggles with lust, right?!) Actually, everything presented within these pages is common-sense stuff. Just ask Ben, a high school student from Minot, North Dakota.

Before getting serious about his pledge to purity, Ben admits to having a serious struggle with lust. Visiting the wrong sites on the Internet and watching certain television shows constantly fueled his battle. "Now when I'm tempted, I pray," he says. "The more I focus on God, the easier it is to win my fight for purity.

"Yet the hardest part is my thought life," he continues. "I have to constantly soak up Scripture and battle in prayer to keep lustful thoughts at bay. Some may say, 'But Ben, you're living in a box.' No, I am striving to live a life worthy of my calling in Christ. Jesus of Nazareth did not visit prostitutes for favors or look lustfully at women. No, the Messiah preached sexual purity and went one step further: He *lived* a life of absolute sexual integrity. The day that I am married, I don't want to have any regrets. The battle is tough, but He is tougher."

Okay. So what exactly is this you're getting into? Is this a devotional? Is it a journal? Is it a *journey*? Actually, yes to all of the above!

In each daily entry you'll find:

- **A TRIBAL QUEST**—a faith challenge for the day.

- **A TRIBAL TRUTH**—Scripture that defines a Christian's tribal creed.

- **A TRIBAL FACE**—a true account of a teen like you or a Bible hero who sought after God's heart and earned himself a new identity in God's worldwide tribe.

- **TRIBAL TRAINING**—advice, action points, and thought-provoking questions and strategies for applying God's truth to your life.

- **TRIBAL MARKS**—a place to jot down your own prayers, thoughts, hopes . . . and all the new stuff you've learned.

So, don't hold back! Fulfill what burns in every young man's heart. Dare to trust your Creator and become the warrior He made you to be. Dare to win the battle for purity.

Use this life-changing resource as a way to get connected to God's eternal tribe. Study with a friend or group of guys from church—maybe even your dad (you know, as your own tribal rite-of-passage thing).

Your ultimate journey awaits. Join the adventure of following Christ. And with each quest He gives you, don't be surprised if you find yourself facing—and overcoming—challenges far greater than anything you ever imagined.

A WARRIOR'S PURITY CREED

I refuse to put myself in situations where I am tempted to compromise my purity.

I commit to the Job Covenant (Job 31:1). I make a covenant with my eye, to keep my mind pure, and not look lustfully at a girl.

I take every thought captive and make it obedient to Christ.

My body is God's temple. I refuse to defile it in any possible way.

I commit to filling my mind and heart with God's Word in order to stay pure (Psalm 119:9).

I commit to having accountability with a few other men of God.

I choose to memorize at least one verse a day that will teach me and train me to be pure and to live a pure life.

I read my commitments to purity every day.

I ask for the Lord's strength and power.

I ask God to keep me from evil and from temptation.

Every time I am tempted, I run to God as fast as I can.

I listen to and read things that encourage me to go after purity.

I don't view purity as a line, but a lifestyle. Purity is my purpose and my pursuit. Because of Jesus I am free, and I use my freedom to become more like Christ and have a heart of purity (John 10:10).

"A Warrior's Purity Creed" is based on Acts 10:15 and was written by 16-year-old Daniel, a Colorado teen who is winning the battle for purity.

A WARRIOR'S BATTLES

BOY TO MAN: UNDERSTANDING THE BATTLE

WEEK 1 ▶▶▶

SURVIVOR SECRETS

▶ ▶ ▶ **WEEKLY MEMORY VERSE**: *Don't let anyone look down on you because you are young, but set an example for the believers in speech, in life, in love, in faith and in purity.* **—1 Timothy 4:12**

TRIBAL QUEST

Accept the truth about your sexuality: Most healthy males have powerful desires for sex. (It's nothing to be ashamed of.) But understand that it's a part of your life that you *must* bring under God's control.

EXPLORE THE WORD: **Galatians 5:16-26**

TRIBAL TRUTH

So I say, live by the Spirit, and you will not gratify the desires of the sinful nature. For the sinful nature desires what is contrary to the Spirit, and the Spirit what is contrary to the sinful nature. They are in conflict with each other, so that you do not do what you want. But if you are led by the Spirit, you are not under law. **—Galatians 5:16-18**

TRIBAL FACE

Josh, 15
Shoreview, Minn.
Striving for Freedom from Lust

Josh sits across the kitchen table from his father, his face strained with sadness. The teen is convinced that God has made a huge mistake with his life.

"I can't stop thinking about sex," he confesses. "It's like, the minute I became a teenager, my brain and my body launched a war against lust. Every day I catch myself having thoughts about girls I know I shouldn't have."

Josh's father nods his head reassuringly and listens.

Josh slumps back in his chair. "But it gets worse."

"You can tell me anything—you do know that, don't you, son?"

Josh looks up and nods. "Of course, but this isn't exactly easy to talk about— especially with my dad."

The teen pauses, trying to muster up courage. Then the words he never imagined telling another soul suddenly roll out of his mouth. "For the past few years, I've had some private struggles," he says. "Stuff I'm ashamed to admit. Stuff like pornography . . . and masturbation."

Josh glances at his father again, fearing condemnation. But instead his eyes are met with compassion.

"You're not alone," his father says. "Many Christian guys share these battles. What sets you apart is your courage to speak up."

"I'm just sick of struggling," Josh says, "and I hate what lust is doing to my relationship with God. I really need help."

Josh then describes three battlegrounds where he has suffered brutal defeat.

BATTLEGROUND 1: Cyberporn

On most weekday nights I don't even bother to switch on the TV. After glancing at my watch, then making some excuse—like having to do algebra and grammatical structures—I leave the dinner table and race upstairs.

I've heard Mom say that she's so "proud of her grown-up son for behaving responsibly and doing his homework." But if she knew what I was really up to, her heart would be broken.

Once upstairs, my actions are anything but responsible—and homework is the last thing on my mind. What I once used as a tool for learning has, lately, become a tool for lust. It's as if cyberporn owns me. And with each click of my mouse, I feel as if I'm being pulled deeper into an evil "web."

BATTLEGROUND 2: Masturbation

My time on the computer is nearly always cut short by a *tap, tap, tap* on my bedroom door, then a friendly voice: "Shut down and hit the sack," Mom tells me. Every night she pokes her head into my room to say good night.

At that point, I'm usually scrambling to maintain my cover. I turn off the monitor, flash a phony smile, and tell an outright lie: "Uhhh—thanks, Mom. Homework's done, and I'm headin' to bed."

When the door shuts behind her, I usually feel like throwing up. *I'm such a hypocrite. I can't continue this double life.*

But when I click off my light and slide between the sheets, my brain replays the images I'd just looked at. Then I get weak and end up giving into another private struggle: masturbation.

BATTLEGROUND 3: Out-of-Control Thought Life

The next morning, I awaken with a knot in my gut. Despite reading a passage of Scripture and praying, feelings of shame add another layer to a wall that's growing higher between Jesus and me.

But by midday the guilt fades, and just being smiled at by a pretty girl churns up a bunch of "mental porn shows." Conversations in the locker room fuel even more messed-up thoughts.

I hear one off-color joke after another—along with crude remarks about sex and body parts. I admit, I even take part in the so-called guy talk.

By the time I arrive home, the ugly lust cycle begins all over again.

Josh looks his father in the eyes. "Dad, I need you to be honest with me," he states sternly. "Am I normal sexually?"

His father grips his son's hand and shares a comforting truth: "Believe it or not, I asked this same question when I was a teen, and here's what my dad told me: 'The average teen guy thinks about sex one minute out of every five—then spends the other four minutes waiting for the one minute to come around again!'"

For a split second, Josh cracks a smile. Then a worried expression washes over his face again. "But this is messed up, Dad—it can't be right. Lust causes so much guilt."

"I didn't say lust is right," his father points out. "I'm telling you that your appetite for sex is a *very normal*, God-given thing. It's your sinful nature that warps what is good. Yet that 'voice' deep inside telling you 'something's wrong' is your conscience . . . and the work of the Holy Spirit."

Suddenly, Josh's father begins to smile, and his eyes seem to sparkle with joy. "I'm so proud of you for hearing that voice," he says. "Too many young men are spiritually deaf. They selfishly focus on what feels good at the moment. But not you! Sensing that something is wrong means that you've already taken the first step toward healing. Now you must take the second step—and many more after that."

Hope replaces the worry on Josh's face. "I'm ready for change," he says. "So, what's next?"

"Prayer," says his father. "Pour out your heart to God. Thank Him for your sexuality, and tell the Lord you want Him to take control of this part of your life. Explain that you're sorry for the sins you've committed, and ask God to heal your heart and to help you change."

Josh nods his head.

Then father and son get on their knees and talk to God.

A huge weight of guilt lifted from Josh's life that day, and the wall he sensed between the Lord and him began to crumble. Yet this young man knows that the battle has just begun. His appetite for sex is stronger than ever, and on occasion, temptation still seems to get the best of him. But Josh isn't about to give up. He knows that he's not alone, which helps him to press on in his fight for purity.

Take a look at another guy—**16-year-old Eric of Dallas, Texas.** Here's how he describes his battles:

> I talk to my dad all of the time about my struggles, and he's very supportive and forgiving. Yet I've still messed up a few times and have surfed Internet porn sites and have fallen into my old habits of fantasizing about sex. Each time after I've lusted, I feel horrible. I promise God that it won't happen again. Then a few days later, I end up doing the same things. I feel like the apostle Paul: "For what I want to do I do not do, but what I hate I do" (Romans 7:15). Sometimes I feel as if I'm in a big hole, and I keep digging in deeper. Yet I'm determined to find freedom from lust.

Why didn't God make the quest for purity easier for guys? Why didn't He give you sexual desires on your wedding night—and not a moment before?

Could it be that our Creator wants to take you on a journey into *authentic masculinity*? I think so. I'm convinced that He wants to embrace that weak, self-centered kid you see in the mirror and transform him into a warrior fit to wear His badge: "a workman approved by God" (see 2 Timothy 2:15).

This transformation—like anything worthwhile in life—involves struggle. Just ask Josh and Eric.

No doubt, you yearn for freedom from lust. (That's why you're reading this book, right?) In the weeks ahead, we'll arm you with some powerful ammunition, as well as a realistic battle plan to strengthen you in your fight for sexual purity. Today, we'll begin with the first crucial steps: (1) cluing into how God wired guys sexually, and (2) striving for self control.

TRIBAL TRAINING

• **Understand the "sex-in-your-head" struggle.** When I sat down to write this book, I counted hundreds of e-mails I've received from guys who feel defeated by lust. Like Josh and Eric, most young men feel alone in their struggles and ashamed of their sexual desires. Yet even though they may be hard to believe, accept these truths: (1) "YOU'RE NORMAL!" and (2) your appetite for sex truly is a good, healthy, God-given thing! The Lord doesn't want you to turn off these desires (as if you could). Instead, He wants to help you control them. How? Keep reading . . .

• **Take an honest look at your sexuality.** In the story above, you read how Josh began to sense that "something's wrong." He knew deep inside that God was working on his heart, pointing out behaviors he needed to change. Allow the Holy Spirit to search your heart today. Get alone and ponder this question: *Do I sense the Lord revealing habits and behaviors in my life that need His healing touch?*

• **Bring your sexual struggles into the light.** Don't try to hide from them. (God already knows what you think and do in private, and He understands your struggles better than you do.) Pray and confess your sins and weaknesses to God. Acknowledge before Him your lack of power to control your sexual urges.

• **Ask God to heal your sexuality, making it the awesome thing He intends it to be.** The key to healthy sexuality is outlined in Scripture. Here's what the apostle Paul wrote in 1 Thessalonians 4:3-5: "It is God's will that you should be sanctified: that you should avoid sexual immorality; that each of you should learn to control his own body in a way that is holy and honorable, not in passionate lust like the heathen, who do not know God." Bottom line: With God's help, every teen boy must seek self-control over his sexuality. Our Lord requires it, girls have a right to it, and above all, it enables you to develop into the godly man you were created to be.

• **Be sincere with your prayers.** Consider this: We will all give account for our choices. This reality actually terrified Paul and motivated him to strive to please God in everything he did (see 2 Corinthians 5:9-11). Christian author Henry Blackaby has also wrestled with this issue. In his book *Experiencing God*, here's what he concludes: "God does not force His will upon us. He will ask us to answer for the way we responded to Him. Christians have been pardoned by the sacrifice of Jesus. We are not condemned. But because God is absolutely just, we will be called on to give an account of our actions."[1]

• **Accept God's forgiveness and stop flogging yourself for your sexual failures.** Persistent guilt and shame will make it difficult to shed sexual problems. (We'll get more into this topic on Days 16 and 17.)

• **PRAY IT OUT: "Lord, I can't do this on my own. Free me from the chains of lust. Heal my sexuality, molding me into the godly man You want me to become."** Pray that He will empower you to avoid temptation to sin by bringing all your sexual thoughts and fantasies under your conscious control. Ask God to remind you when your thoughts need controlling.

▶▶▶CONSIDER TAKING TO HEART THIS PRAYER FROM RICHARD FOSTER:

Lord Jesus Christ, when I read the gospel stories, I am touched by Your healing power. You healed sick bodies to be sure, but You did so much more. You healed the spirit and the deep, inner mind. Most of all, I am touched by Your actions of acceptance that spoke healing into those who lived on the margins of life, shoved aside by the strong and the powerful.

Speak Your healing into me, Lord, body and mind and soul. Most of all, heal my sense of worthlessness. My head tells me that I am of infinite value to You, but my heart cannot believe it. Heal my heart, Jesus, heal my heart. Amen.

TRIBAL MARKS

A KEY POINT I LEARNED TODAY:

_____

_____

_____

_____

_____

_____

HOW I WANT TO GROW:

_____

_____

_____

_____

_____

MY PRAYER LIST:

_____

_____

_____

_____

_____

_____

SURVIVOR SECRETS

▶▶▶**WEEKLY MEMORY VERSE**: *Don't let anyone look down on you because you are young, but set an example for the believers in speech, in life, in love, in faith and in purity.* —1 Timothy 4:12

TRIBAL QUEST

Trust that saving sex for marriage is God's perfect plan for your life—despite what your peers may believe.

EXPLORE THE WORD: —Colossians 3:1-10

TRIBAL TRUTH

Put to death, therefore, whatever belongs to your earthly nature: sexual immorality, impurity, lust, evil desires and greed, which is idolatry.
—Colossians 3:5

TRIBAL FACE

Ryan, 16
Amarillo, Texas
Locker-Room Slam

"She's so hot!" Matt says as he pulls off his practice jersey. He flings it into his locker, then pelts Ryan with a sweaty sock. "And she's going out with a dweeb like YOU!"

"Unreal," Chris chimes in. "If I dated her . . . ooohhh, dude. . . ." He falls to the floor, clutching his chest—faking a massive coronary.

Jason grins at Ryan. "So, you've been going out with her for a few weeks, huh?! Just what happens when you two are alone—totally alone?"

Ryan shrugs. "You know, stuff. We talk, watch TV . . ."

"*And*," Jason presses.

"Eat, study, talk some more . . ."

PLOP! THUD! SMACK!

The guys bomb Ryan with crusted gym clothes. Then Matt launches the ultimate question: "Give us all the details, dude. Has she let you have it yet?"

Ryan looks up and swallows, sirens blazing in his head: *GEEK ALERT*—

COOLNESS ABOUT TO BE CRUSHED.

"Ahhh . . . have what?" he asks nonchalantly (knowing full well which "it" his friend is referring to).

"'IT,' you idiot," Matt barks. "Whadda ya think?"

Of course, Ryan had never done it, and he wasn't going to—until marriage. In his eyes, moving too fast too soon spelled major headaches: pregnancy, sexual diseases, broken hearts. And as a committed Christian, he had an even better reason to wait: It was God's will for his life.

But the guys. . . . How on earth could he explain that to them?

Ryan looks Matt in the eye. "And I suppose *you* have?!"

Matt bristles. "Course I've done it . . . lots of times. What *normal* guy hasn't?"

Ryan's stomach knots up. He hates locker-room talk—especially when his reputation is on the line. He doesn't want to lie, BUT . . .

"Well . . . ahhh . . ." Ryan pauses. "Actually I . . . or I mean we . . . ahhh . . ." (His internal "geek alert" suddenly reaches critical status.)

What do I tell them? he wonders as he frantically searches for the precise words. *How do I stand for what's right without being laughed at . . . and without looking like a total idiot?*

There's no escape.

Hang out in the locker room or the halls at school—even some church youth groups—and you hear guys bragging about the so-called good times they have with girls.

Flip on the tube or crack open a magazine and someone's selling a lie about sex.

Step into some public restrooms and . . . Huh? . . . a strange little box on the wall conveniently offers condoms (that is, if you have some quarters to spare).

All this leads you to believe that waiting is just plain *weird*.

Guess what? Despite the sex-on-credit, play-now-pay-later culture we live in, not everyone is doing it. Lots of teens are saving up for good sex—when it's *really* safe and *really* right.

Take the thousands who marched in the national capitals of Canada and the United States. Proud of their virginity—and not afraid to admit it—many signed "True Love Waits" cards.

Then more than 210,000 of these cards were displayed in Washington, D.C., and Ottawa as a visual representation of teenagers all over the world who have made a pact for purity.

Yet do you catch yourself relating to Ryan—wondering if you're the only virgin left on the planet, and even feeling a little weird for waiting? Let's tune in to the truth and uncover the gutsy commitments God expects from His tribe.

TRIBAL TRAINING

• **Know God's design for sex.** It's designed for only one kind of committed relationship: holy matrimony. When a husband and a wife have sexual intercourse, something happens to the two of them, something that changes them at the deepest level. A man and a woman are bound together body and soul. And this bond is never supposed to be separated. (Can you see why divorce is so devastating?)

In other words, sex isn't just physical, and it's not a trivial act that feels good for a few seconds and then is over for good. Sex involves a couple's bodies, minds, and emotions in an activity that is intended to continue for a lifetime.

• **Learn what the Bible says.** Because it does not say the exact words, "Don't have sex before marriage" in the Bible, some guys try to argue that premarital sex must be okay. Yet the Bible does clearly communicate that premarital sex equals sin.

A number of passages in the Bible tell us that marriage is the right place for sex—and *specifically* state that extramarital alternatives are off-limits for believers. Take a look:

Adultery is wrong—Exodus 20:14
Sex with a prostitute is wrong—1 Corinthians 6:15-17
Impurity is wrong—Colossians 3:5-7
Marriage is a sacred bond—Hebrews 13:4

With verses such as these, is it possible that God would condone sex outside of marriage?

• **Take some advice from a "big brother."** Check out the following letter. It's from a guy who has "been there, done that"—and desperately wishes he hadn't. Eighteen-year-old Sean of Grand Rapids, Michigan, sent it to me, along with a request: "Please print this so other guys can hear the truth, and maybe avoid the mistakes I've made."

I have something important to say to every teen guy out there. I'm an 18-year-old who has always heard Christian views about premarital sex and the consequences of giving in. Unfortunately, I didn't listen. It seems that the whole world is telling us that sex is okay. And it is—strictly within the bonds of marriage. But instead of following God's Word, I tuned in to the world and gave away my virginity.

At the time, I was convinced that having sex was the most wonderful thing in the world. Afterward, it left both the girl and me with heartache. I don't mean simple hurt feelings; I'm talking about utter heartache. Not a day goes by that I don't regret that first sexual touch. Why? Because it gradually led to other things— and eventually to intercourse.

I know that God has forgiven me for my sins, but I can't help asking myself, *Will my future wife forgive me? How am I going to tell her that I gave away a gift that was meant only for her?* And on my wedding night, I'll have pictures of other girls in my head, which is so wrong! To treat women as most of the secular world does is absolute sin.

Fellas, I envy every one of you who doesn't know what sexual intimacy with a girl is like. If you're a virgin, you are so fortunate. I pray that you'll stay pure for marriage and that God will richly bless your marriage bed. And as much as you want sex now, remember that God has the right kind of woman in mind for you. Hold strong and give your future wife the gift of your virginity.

• **PRAY IT OUT: "Lord, I'm committed to purity."** Ask Jesus for the strength to stand strong in the face of pressure. Tell Him you want to save yourself sexually for your future wife.

TRIBAL MARKS

A KEY POINT I LEARNED TODAY:

_____

_____

_____

_____

_____

_____

HOW I WANT TO GROW:

_____

_____

_____

_____

_____

_____

MY PRAYER LIST:

_____

_____

_____

_____

_____

_____

SURVIVOR SECRETS

▶▶▶**WEEKLY MEMORY VERSE**: *Don't let anyone look down on you because you are young, but set an example for the believers in speech, in life, in love, in faith and in purity.* **—1 Timothy 4:12**

TRIBAL QUEST

The lies about sex are many—and they've been around for centuries. Learn to recognize those lies, and you're on your way to victory.

EXPLORE THE WORD: **Proverbs 7:1-27**

TRIBAL TRUTH

With persuasive words she led him astray; she seduced him with her smooth talk. All at once he followed her like an ox going to the slaughter, like a deer stepping into a noose. **—Proverbs 7:21-22**

TRIBAL FACE

Dave, 20
Engaged to Be Married

Despite being so young, Dave had found the girl of his dreams and was engaged to be married. He'd never slept with a girl, but in his mind he was no virgin. Pornography had been a problem on and off since he was 12.

Now that he was engaged to a wonderful Christian woman, Dave wanted to do right, live pure, honor JESUS, and treat her like a lady. With the memories of a dark past, he knew it was going to be tough. So, Dave had a let's-define-the-relationship talk with his bride-to-be.

"Honey, I don't think we should kiss until the wedding rehearsal. Let's just keep it to holding hands for now."

She was 19, beautiful, and wanted to serve Jesus. She, too, was a virgin, but for years she had dreamed about her first kiss. Now that a ring sparkled on her finger, this still-waiting-for-my-first-kiss thing was hard to take.

"What if we make fools of ourselves at the rehearsal?" she asked.

Dave fielded that question as best he could.

"How am I supposed to know you truly love me by just holding hands?"

Dave took a while answering that one.

"I don't want to wait," she insisted. "I want to kiss you now."

Dave held out for a few more days, but the words *I want to kiss you now* kept haunting him. Finally, sadly, he dispensed with the hold-hands-until-the-rehearsal idea. They kissed. They liked it.

Arms and necks interlocked, they kissed some more.

Hollywood would have thought, *Boring*. But the passions Dave experienced that night unlocked a huge desire mixed with a host of lies. Each lie brought the relationship one step closer to complete ruin.

One day she said, "I don't think you love me. All you ever want to do is *kiss*." She spat the last word like poison. Her bitterness ran deep. Having thrown away the boundaries, they had "kissed" far more than each other's lips. She almost gave him back the ring.

Dave wanted to scream that it wasn't his idea to kiss in the first place. But he didn't. Dave knew that being the relationship's leader, he'd made bad choices. He couldn't blame her.

The couple backed off to cooler, more manageable boundaries. They stopped kissing, but the scars were there. Scars don't go away.

When the wedding day came, technically Dave and his bride were still virgins. But as "technical virgins" on the most special day of their lives, they didn't feel too special. They had acted like impatient children at Christmas. The gift of sex had been partially unwrapped. When they finished unwrapping it the night they got married, it wasn't much of a surprise.

Years later, Dave still feels the sting of his wrong choices. With the clarity of hindsight, here are a few of the lies he believed:

Since we'll be married soon anyway, no one will know.

This bold-faced lie is crazy. First off, having a baby five months after your wedding is kind of a giveaway.

Assuming that doesn't happen (a huge, foolish assumption), you've still got problems. No one will know? Yeah, right. The second you cross the line, four persons will instantly be aware of your bad choice.

First, you.

Second, her.

Third, Satan.

Fourth, God.

First, you. This side of heaven, you cannot and will not forget the sexual compromises you've made. Sex is so much a part of your soul, its memory burns itself into your hard drive, never to be erased.

Proverbs 6:28 asks an important question: "Can a man walk on hot coals without his feet being scorched?" Can you have illicit sex without scars? The two questions are one and the same. You may have sexual scars already. Want more?

The choice is yours.

Second, she. Sexual sin has a way of destroying the closest relationships. She may forgive you. You may even get married. But she will never forget your failure to lead the relationship in purity. It will always be a thorn in the memory of your love, a blight in your history as her man. Is the feeling of a moment worth the reputation of a lifetime?

That should be a no-brainer.

Third, Satan. Satan and his hosts know when you've compromised your purity. Having seen your sexual compromise, Satan will be accusing you—long after you've moved on. And when you're feeling destroyed and abandoned by God, then you won't care about deeper sin, will you?

Ever felt the sting of the devil's accusations?

Want more?

Fourth, God. God groans every time His children fall into sin, particularly sexual sin (Ephesians 4:30). Satan's accusations may sting the soul's surface, but the groan of God will rumble the very core of your being. God's deep grief for the hurt you're inflicting upon yourself is a grief you can live without.

When she says "no," she means "yes."

The danger of this lie is that it borders on truth.

Just like you, women are created to enjoy intimacy. Sometimes by saying no, a woman might simply mean, "slow down." But not always. And certainly not when she's thinking clearly. Females do like the buildup, just like you, but that's no excuse to play with fire and take advantage.

Think of the Person living inside that girl (Galatians 2:20). While you're sitting on that cozy love seat, her "no" really means "no," because you both reflect the One living in your souls.

What does the Bible say on the subject of sex before marriage? "Flee!" (1 Corinthians 6:18). Regardless what your body tells you—or hers, for that matter—God is the only One to whom you should be listening.

His is the voice of reason, and He always says what He means.

"True love" makes sex before marriage acceptable.

Doesn't it bug you that Adam and Eve didn't have to wait? They loved each other; they made love. No waiting for the wedding, no mailing invitations, or messing with flower arrangements.

But God intended the sanctity of marriage (one man sleeping with one woman for life) to be formally honored by a ceremonial wedding. Joseph and Mary had a similar waiting period in their culture, only Joseph had to wait even longer because of the unique circumstances around Jesus' birth. (Poor guy.) They eventually had at least six children together (Mark 6:3). (Lucky guy.) But they did so only after following the obligations of marriage in Jewish culture. Before that, Joseph never touched Mary.

The strongest emotions and sensations of love do not constitute a marriage. You get that only at the altar. Nor are the goose bumps of passion a license to nibble on the "wedding cake" six weeks before the big day. The fact that your passions are burning may make you want to change your mind on a three-year engagement period and get married sooner (1 Corinthians 7:9)—but the "cake" only means something once you've been to the wedding.

"Masculinity" must be expressed; it cannot be controlled.

Imagine a young, unmarried couple in the backseat of a car at night with a panoramic view of a quiet construction site, their bodies aflame.

"Baby, you're so incredible. I can't help myself."

You can picture it, can't you? In that moment, Satan's lie seems true: Masculinity cannot be controlled.

Now picture this: Someone taps the window of the car. The young man spins around and stares through the steamy window—into the angry eyes of his girlfriend's father. All of a sudden, the young man discovers that he can control himself.

He'd better. His manly neck is on the line.

Though your flesh may scream that it can't be controlled—something Paul himself experienced (Romans 7)—there is a solution: Jesus (Romans 6).

In fact, you can control your passions. Loose passions and STDs make a to-die-for combination these days. At the very least, the quality of your spiritual life (way more important than your physical life) is on the line.

Jesus will forgive us, so let's enjoy.

The fact that Jesus forgives sexual sin is an important, unchanging truth. Ex-prostitutes who have come to know Him can tell you the wonders of Christ's forgiveness.

But that's not the only truth that comes into play on the subject of sexual sin. Try Galatians 6:7-8 on for size: "Do not be deceived: God cannot be mocked. A man reaps what he sows. The one who sows to please his sinful nature, from that nature will reap destruction."

As your Savior, Jesus does forgive. As God, Jesus will not be mocked. If you play games with His blood-bought forgiveness, you're gambling for a mountain of hurt.

TRIBAL TRAINING

• **List the lies.** Write down all the lies you've believed regarding sex. Take your time, and put them in plain English. Root out the devil's sales pitches and stare at them on paper.

• **Copy down truths from God's Word**—especially ones that slash those lies to pieces. Dwell on them. Savor them.

• **Create new goals**—actions—that will enable you to act in accordance with the new truths on which you're meditating. Be specific. Make your list measurable, items you can check off. "Burn that magazine I have hidden under the bed," is a good example of a measurable goal. "Be pure for the rest of my life," though a desirable aim, is NOT a measurable goal. Desirable aims are reached through measurable goals, tiny steps leading to a great destination.

• **Check off each goal as it's accomplished.** And when you're done with the list, try the cycle again. Keep a record of your spiritual progress in a journal. Let God encourage you on paper.

• **PRAY IT OUT: "Lord, help me to avoid the lies about sex."** Tell Jesus you desire sexual purity. Ask Him to help you make this goal a reality.

TRIBAL MARKS

A KEY POINT I LEARNED TODAY:

_____

_____

_____

_____

_____

_____

HOW I WANT TO GROW:

_____

_____

_____

_____

_____

_____

MY PRAYER LIST:

_____

_____

_____

_____

_____

_____

_____

SURVIVOR SECRETS

▶ ▶ ▶ **WEEKLY MEMORY VERSE**: *Don't let anyone look down on you because you are young, but set an example for the believers in speech, in life, in love, in faith and in purity.* —1 Timothy 4:12

TRIBAL QUEST

Understand that lust and love are opposites, especially when it comes to sex. We'll learn the difference using the life of David as a prime example.

EXPLORE THE WORD: 2 Samuel 11:1-12:14

TRIBAL TRUTH

When tempted, no one should say, "God is tempting me." For God cannot be tempted by evil, nor does he tempt anyone; but each one is tempted when, by his own evil desire, he is dragged away and enticed. Then, after desire has conceived, it gives birth to sin; and sin, when it is full-grown, gives birth to death. —James 1:13-15

TRIBAL FACE

David

A King Defeated by Lust

David was a king, the king of Israel. On a day when he should have been doing the kingly thing—leading his people into battle—he sloughed off the job on his top general, Joab, and loafed around the palace. Bored out of his royal gourd, he climbed up to the palace roof and had a look around.

Then he did a double take.

That's one fine naked lady! What was her name again? Bathsheba? Wife of Uriah? I'm getting her up here right now.

Ever have something similar happen while loafing around the den, channel surfing?

Idleness and lust go hand in hand. Count on it. If you're lazing around, with no clear direction about what to do with your day, the door to lust easily swings wide open. Sit down in front of your high-speed Internet connection with that same attitude, and you're inviting lust to come right on in.

First, let's talk about lust. Then we'll look at idleness.

Lust and love have only one thing in common. They both can be expressed via sex. After that, the similarities end.

Lust is from your own sinful nature, often enhanced by the urgings of Satan. Love, true love, is a gift from God, a fruit of His Spirit living within you.

Lust is impatient; it demands immediate gratification. Love knows how to wait.

Lust looks only at the outside: the lips, the hair, the wiggle. Love looks within: the character, the hurts, the joys.

Lust is rough, demanding. Love is gentle, considerate.

Lust throws in the towel on relationships as soon as the problems outweigh the pleasure. Love knows how to stand true in a 60-year marriage of inevitable ups and downs.

Lust is self-centered; it seeks only to get. When lust pretends to give a little, it's always in order to get more. Love, on the other hand, always looks for ways to give, and it's sincere, with no personal agenda, no "rewards program" in mind. When love expresses itself within the boundaries of marriage, it seeks her pleasure first—and that may take all week! Many married men have yet to learn the difference between love and lust, even with their wives. If you could learn this important distinction, you'll be miles ahead when God gives you that wonderful woman.

Meanwhile, you've got some time ahead of you. How are you going to spend it? If you haven't planned how you're going to spend your day, Satan's got a few ideas for you: *Why don't you just mosey over to that lounge chair and pick up the J.C. Penney catalog? Lingerie isn't pornography. It's art. It's God's creation wrapped in lace.*

Idleness is the devil's favorite playground.

Loafing around, wasting time, was King David's first mistake. Then came adultery and murder. Sexual sin is the default mode of a man with nothing to do.

Now here's the secret: You avoid the first mistake—time with nothing to do—and you can avoid the immoral mistakes that follow. If you become allergic to being idle, you'll dismiss the majority of testosterone temptations that come from living as a guy on Planet Earth.

Ever realize that as a follower of Jesus Christ, you are a soldier? Check out 2 Timothy 2:3-4. You've got battles to fight, cities to conquer. You don't have *10 seconds* to be muddling around like some hobo with a finger up his nose. God made you a warrior, a commando for Christ. You have a life full of important missions and cool assignments to fulfill (Ephesians 2:10). When you catch a glimpse of the great, celestial, eternal wonder it is to be a soldier for the King of kings, you won't have a second to spare for J.C. Penney.

So, make the decision: *Idleness, in my life, you're dead. I'm going to get active, stay active, and enjoy the fruits of an active existence. I'm going to concentrate on figuring out what God wants me to do—in great detail and on paper—and then I'm going to do it.*

I'm a warrior. I'm moving forward, ready to conquer.

TRIBAL TRAINING

• **Become a goal-oriented person.** I (Manfred) once spent ten hours writing 100 goals for my life. For me, it was a great time for change. That list, and the whole goal-oriented mentality that came with it, gave me the change I desperately needed. Why? Because now I find myself asking, with pen in hand: "What do You want me to do today, Lord? How should I spend my time?" And writing down what I feel He's saying makes it a whole lot more likely to happen. Goals are great. Writing them down is even better.

• **Keep a journal of the goals God puts on your heart.** Record the dates when you see them accomplished. Enjoy reviewing your journal, thanking Jesus for being there as you accomplished each item.

• **Remember: Satan is a mere prince.** (See Ephesians 2:2.) You don't have to serve him anymore. You know Someone with more clout, the King of the universe, and you report directly to Him. You don't have time for Satan. You're too busy soldiering for your King.

• **PRAY IT OUT: "Lord, help me battle the lust beast."** Ask Jesus to guard your heart and to guide your steps.

▶▶▶ CONSIDER TAKING TO HEART THIS PRAYER FROM SAINT AUGUSTINE:

O God, our true life, to know you is life, to serve you is freedom, to enjoy you is a kingdom, to praise you is the joy and happiness of the soul. I praise and bless and adore you, I worship you, I glorify you. I give thanks to you for your great glory. I humbly beg you to live with me, to reign in me, to make this heart of mine a holy temple, a fit habitation for your divine majesty.

TRIBAL MARKS

A KEY POINT I LEARNED TODAY:

_____

_____

_____

_____

_____

_____

HOW I WANT TO GROW:

_____

_____

_____

_____

_____

_____

MY PRAYER LIST:

_____

_____

_____

_____

_____

_____

_____

SURVIVOR SECRETS

▶▶▶ **WEEKLY MEMORY VERSE**: *Don't let anyone look down on you because you are young, but set an example for the believers in speech, in life, in love, in faith and in purity.* —1 Timothy 4:12

TRIBAL QUEST

Stop drowning in guilt, secrecy, and self-condemnation over masturbation and begin applying God's transforming wisdom to this battle.

EXPLORE THE WORD: Ephesians 5:1-14

TRIBAL TRUTH

But among you there must not be even a hint of sexual immorality, or of any kind of impurity, or of greed, because these are improper for God's holy people. —Ephesians 5:3

TRIBAL FACE

**Teen Tribal Trekkers
and Their Campfire Conversation**

Fifteen-year-old Will of Dallas, Texas, feels defeated. "I'm a Christian," he says, "but I get so caught up in the things of the flesh—especially lustful thoughts. I feel as if my faith has lost its fire, and I feel distant from God."

Sam, 14, nods his head in agreement and adds to the conversation. "Lust is like a beast that takes over. I get weak and I give in to its power—thinking and doing things that seem anything but Christian."

It's day five of *Breakaway's* weeklong backpacking trip near Yosemite, California, and the guys in my tribe are opening up to each other. In addition to my responsibilities as the magazine's editor, my team and I take boys on faith-building wilderness adventures in California and Colorado. (Flip to the back of this book for information on these summer excursions.)

As our campfire conversation heats up, the masks come off, and the guys begin to share their deepest fears and struggles.

"I'm with Sam," says David, 17, from Placentia, California. "The lust beast causes me to do some pretty shameful stuff." He suddenly pauses. Despite the crackling fire, David feels cold and empty inside. Every muscle seems to tremble. He looks down and tries to blink away the tears.

"I don't think you guys are going to respect me anymore when I tell you my biggest battle," David continues. "But I feel like I need to confess it to you. So, I may as well just say it: I struggle with masturbation."

Most of the twelve guys sitting around the campfire actually look relieved by David's confession—not shocked. The boys hang on every word as their friend tells his story: "It's been a secret problem for, like, five years now," David says. "But I've never told anyone. It's like I'm addicted to masturbation. I can't stop myself, yet I feel so horrible afterward. I constantly cry out to God, telling Him I'm sorry—and promising that it'll never happen again. But then it does."

Suddenly, Sam speaks up: "I respect you more, David, for being honest. It takes guts to talk about this. And just so you know, I struggle, too. But my dad tells me not to sweat it. He says it's not a sin and that every guy deals with masturbation."

At this point, 16-year-old Luke—who has remained silent the whole evening—groans and slumps back on the ground. All eyes turn toward him.

"What's wrong?" Sam asks. "Do you disagree with me?"

Luke sits up and scrunches his forehead. "Yes—and no," he says. "I agree that every guy deals with masturbation, but I disagree that we 'shouldn't sweat it.' My church teaches that masturbation is a sin, like anything else related to lust."

Will chimes in, shaking his head. "So, your church automatically labels *masturbation* as a form of *lust*?" he asks.

"Of course," Luke says. "How can it be anything else? I mean, when you do it, you're not exactly thinking about innocent things."

A couple of guys snicker nervously. Luke continues sharing his thoughts. "My pastor says that masturbation invites the sins of lust and fantasy. So, I've been taught to avoid it completely. It's difficult, but I know it's a powerful exercise in self-control. Avoiding masturbation wards off other lustful temptations."

"Luke, you have my respect, too," Sam says. "And I agree that masturbation can invite the sins of lust, but I believe it doesn't have to. My dad—and my pastor— describe masturbation as a way to 'release sexual pressure' in order to stay pure."

Will agrees. "I confessed that I give in to lust, but I wasn't talking about masturbation," he says. "I was referring to the 'mental porn shows' that invade my brain. It sounds weird, but I believe masturbation can be a kind of a mechanical act, without fantasy. I think it can be a way of releasing sexual pressure without sinning."

The glowing embers in the campfire pop and crackle, and the group gets silent. Each guy ponders the different views on the issue.

David looks up at the infinite canopy of stars and begins to pray. "So, who's right, God? Is masturbation a sin—or is it okay? Can it be disconnected from lust?"

Where do you stand on the issue of masturbation? Do you relate to Luke and believe that abstaining is the best approach? Or, like Sam, do you view it as a harmless way of releasing sexual pressure?

Then again, maybe you're somewhere in the middle. Perhaps, like David, you're confused and torn up over this issue. You're not quite comfortable doing it, yet you feel it's next to impossible to stop.

As we discussed in Days 1 and 2, God created you with a wonderful and appropriate desire for the opposite sex. Sure, these impulses are strong. But someday, when you're married, you'll be able to celebrate and satisfy these desires with a woman you love. This is all part of God's incredible plan.

But in the meantime, what's a guy to do? And if you're not alone in your battle with masturbation, why are so many churches silent about it? Why are most Christians like David confused?

Despite our culture's preoccupation with sex, our sexuality and sexual development are very private, personal matters. And historically, there have been a lot of myths and scary facts floating around, or even being taught, about masturbation. But maybe the biggest silencer is guilt. Satan loves to heap it on, and he'd love to use it to drive a wedge between you and God.

As you probably already know, when masturbation becomes a habit, it brings with it feelings of guilt and shame. Are these feelings from God? Does this mean that regular masturbation is sin?

This whole subject would be much easier if there were a Bible verse that said, "thou shalt not," or "verily, it is okay." But the Bible is silent on this issue. While there are those who claim Genesis 38:8-11 condemns Onan for masturbation and that 1 Corinthians 6:9-10 refers to this habit, the Bible scholars we've talked with believe these arguments are taken completely out of context.

We certainly don't want to contradict what your parents or your pastor teaches. But weigh the insights, the relevant scriptures, and differing perspectives. Then pray and ask God to reveal His will for you in your particular case.

• **Don't think of yourself as weird.** You've learned in today's lesson that many other Christian guys struggle with this, too. So, don't feel strange for having a desire to masturbate. Also, if you don't struggle—keep in mind that there's nothing wrong with you, either.

• **Gain the right perspective.** Considering that masturbation is not specifically mentioned in the Bible, we can conclude it shouldn't be given special focus. Yet a lot of Christian guys would put masturbation as one of the most significant battles in their attempt to live as Christians. Still, if God doesn't consider it worth significant discussion, you certainly shouldn't let guilt drive you away from Him.

• **Understand the real problems:** guilt, addiction, hidden fears, and destructive myths. Masturbation will not cause blindness, weakness, or mental retardation, and it won't cause a guy to lose his ability to father a child in the future. The best way to avoid problems with masturbation is to open up and discuss this issue with a trusted adult—preferably your dad.

• **Avoid the danger zones.**
Masturbation can be harmful and should be avoided if it's done . . .
. . . while fantasizing about an immoral relationship (see Matthew 5:27-28).
. . . with pornography or any other "unclean picture" set before your eyes.
. . . to the point of becoming an addiction. If it's getting in the way of your living your life, or if it's causing difficulty in your relationships, you should talk with someone.

• **Strive for sexual self-control.** I don't think there's anything necessarily wrong with thinking about sex. (It's kind of hard to avoid, right?) But I do believe every male's sexual imagination has to be controlled. Why? Many guys who masturbate harbor fantasies that are plainly immoral. Again, these should have no place in a Christian's life. What's more, the discipline of bringing your sex drive under control will help you to be a healthier, more fulfilled, godly person. So, what do I mean by self-control?

1. Avoid the danger zones listed above.

2. Strive to remain otherwise occupied every day, consciously striving to go for longer and longer times between relapses (remembering not to give in to guilt and celebrating your achievements).

3. Steer clear of mental porn shows. (Day 15 goes deeper into this.)

4. Use the following verse as a shield—even repeat it in the face of temptation: "Flee from sexual immorality. . . . You are not your own; you were bought at a price. Therefore honor God with your body" (1 Corinthians 6:18-20).

• Take to heart some expert advice.

DR. JAMES DOBSON: "It is my opinion that masturbation is not much of an issue with God. It's a normal part of adolescence, which involves no one else. It does not cause disease, it does not produce babies, and Jesus did not mention it in the Bible. I'm not telling you to masturbate, and I hope you won't feel the need for it. The best thing I can do is suggest that you talk to God personally about this matter and decide what He wants you to do."

DR. WALT LARIMORE: "Putting images in your mind that are sexual—like sexually explicit TV shows, Web sites, videos, or magazines—or thinking wrongly about girls at school is what the Bible calls lust. And Scripture is clear that we are to flee or run from lust and sexual immorality. Boys who choose not to dwell on impure thoughts may find it easier not to masturbate, not because masturbation is bad or a sin, but because these boys don't want the impure thoughts they have while they are masturbating."

• PRAY IT OUT: "Lord, I need Your guidance with the issue of masturbation." Talk to God honestly about this struggle. He understands what you are going through. Tell Him how you feel, and ask Him for the strength to be self-controlled sexually. Ask God to help you steer clear of lust and immoral sexual fantasies.

TRIBAL MARKS

A KEY POINT I LEARNED TODAY:

_____

_____

_____

_____

_____

_____

HOW I WANT TO GROW:

_____

_____

_____

_____

_____

_____

MY PRAYER LIST:

_____

_____

_____

_____

_____

_____

SURVIVOR SECRETS

▶▶▶ **WEEKLY MEMORY VERSE**: *Don't let anyone look down on you because you are young, but set an example for the believers in speech, in life, in love, in faith and in purity.* —**1 Timothy 4:12**

TRIBAL QUEST

Know that men and women simply are not born homosexual. God did not design us this way.

EXPLORE THE WORD: **Romans 1:18-32**

TRIBAL TRUTH

For although they knew God, they neither glorified him as God nor gave thanks to him, but their thinking became futile and their foolish hearts were darkened. —**Romans 1:21**

TRIBAL FACE

Dark Desires: A Teen Guy's Struggle with Homosexuality

While I receive hundreds of e-mails each month from teen guys, the one I've reprinted here really tugged at my heart. It was from a young man who was struggling with homosexuality, and his story was a bit graphic.

As you read it, keep in mind that his painful journey represents the kinds of difficult sexual issues with which you and your peers are grappling.

Likewise, my response to him—which I organized under "Tribal Training"— illustrates the type of open dialogue we need to have. Sweeping tough questions under the carpet just won't do. We must hear biblical truth, and we can't hold back from sharing it.

I've lost so much sleep over this during the past few months. I feel sick and twisted and dirty. I'm literally torn up inside—so full of shame, guilt, and confusion.

How could I let this happen? Why am I attracted to something so dark? I'd give anything to go back and change my actions.

I'm a Christian, so I know my Creator did not make me homosexual. I've prayed and cried—yet I just can't seem to let go of my unthinkable desires. I don't want to hurt my friend, but I'm dying spiritually. What we do in secret has to stop.

That's why I'm writing you this letter in the middle of the night. I don't necessarily want a reply as much as I need to let everything out. If you don't have time to read a lengthy e-mail about a stranger's spiritual battles, then just delete all of this, and pray for me. *Please, please pray for me.*

It really helps just knowing that someone else in the world has heard my struggle. It gives me hope to think that someone is praying for me.

The thing I'm most ashamed of happened a few summers ago—when I was 16. Yet the steps that got me to that ugly point happened years earlier.

I really hit it off with a guy in youth group. It seemed that we had a lot in common (more than I ever imagined). We decided to attend a weeklong church camp together and agreed to be roommates in a dorm unit.

While at camp one day, we started talking about sexual stuff. I thought this was what guys did all the time when they're around each other, Christian or not. But before we knew it, our talk got twisted and gross. And in the days that followed, our filthy "bantering" led to experimentation. Suddenly, I found myself doing things with this guy that were shameful.

Is it what I've feared for a long time? Am I really homosexual? I wondered afterward.

My new friend admitted that he struggled with homosexual desires. He explained that his male cousin had raped him when he was eight years old, which had caused confusion with his sexual identity. He also said that he didn't want to force anything on me.

I told him that I didn't have any regrets. And during our last few days at camp—a place we'd come to deepen our faith—I ended up turning my back on God. Instead, I gave in to my carnal side. And in the years that followed, long after the trip was behind me, I continued to "see" this friend.

Then it happened: God brought me back to my senses.

Recently one morning, I looked in the mirror and broke down. I sensed in my heart that my actions were wrong. I felt God's conviction, and I knew I had to confess, repent, and run far away from these sins.

Yet I didn't pray or take those steps.

I felt confused and paralyzed. Part of me was afraid of the fierce spiritual battle ahead. My other side didn't want to give up these strange new experiences. I'd never really felt loved, and I certainly didn't receive any attention from girls. All my life I'd been called "ugly," "fat," and "disgusting." And that was how I felt about myself. Yet here was someone who actually found me physically attractive.

I also had another struggle that held me back. It was a problem that had fueled my confusion all these years: I was addicted to Internet pornography—both straight and otherwise (especially *otherwise*). In addition, I often talked to homosexual men in chat rooms.

So, this brings me to the dilemma I face today. I feel so hypocritical and worthless. My life is out of control, and I feel as if Satan has a hold on me. I can't seem to break free.

Sexual desire floods my mind all the time—which I know is fairly normal for an 18-year-old. Yet I keep having homosexual fantasies, and I live from day to day with regret and guilt.

I love God, I really do. I want to serve Him and get out of this mess I've made of my life. I want to start over; I just don't know how. And to be honest, I don't want to talk to a pastor or counselor because I'm so ashamed. I especially don't want all my closest friends to know. Yes, the consequences of my actions have trickled down and hurt more people than I can count. I'm just so lost and confused.

I'll end with what I asked at the beginning of this letter: *Please, please pray for me.*

Trapped, confused, hopeless—words that describe this young man's dilemma. He says he feels "out of control" and fears that Satan has a hold on him. Sadly, he's right.

The enemy has fed him lies and does, in fact, have a firm grip on his life. Yet, through the power of Jesus Christ, this young man can break free. Despite his trapped feeling, there is hope.

In fact, he repeatedly points to the answer in his letter: prayer. Turning to God with a sincere heart is the first step toward healing, transformation—and a way out of darkness. The second step is the one he resists: getting professional help.

While the story above may seem extreme, the number of Christian guys who struggle with similar fears and desires seems to be growing. Check out this letter to Breakaway that echoes similar e-mails sent to our magazine:

For years I have struggled with gay thoughts and feelings. I know the Bible is totally against homosexuality, and I don't want to be gay, anyway. Satan has just really got a hold on me. I've asked the Lord for help, but I still feel the devil's hand pulling me down. Are there other Christians guys going through the same thing? How do I stop these feelings and thoughts? Help!

Even if you don't relate to today's lesson, God may one day count on you to help a struggling friend.

TRIBAL TRAINING

• **Same-sex feelings don't make you gay.** The conflicting emotions you're experiencing, as well as the questions about yourself and your feelings toward the opposite sex are a normal part of growing up for many, if not most boys. Rest assured: It's perfectly normal for teen sexual desires to range far and wide.

• **Acting upon same-sex desires is sin.** Prayer is the primary defense in this battle. But realize your feelings will probably not go away overnight. And opening up doors in your thought life or through your actions with others could potentially fuel your confusion, as well as the depth of your struggle.

• **Know that _gay_ does not describe who a person is.** The word _gay_ is a political term that describes a chosen lifestyle. Despite the "evidence" you may have heard, men and women simply are not born homosexual. God did not design us this way. In fact, the Lord makes it clear that homosexuality is a sinful choice—and He even describes it as unnatural and indecent (see Romans 1:21-32 and 1 Corinthians 6:9-11).

• **Get help.** Don't struggle alone. Breaking free from same-sex attraction can be a difficult endeavor, one that requires commitment, perseverance, and a strong relationship with the Lord. Focus on the Family's Web site (www.family. org) offers a number of resources. Also, there's a fantastic Christian Web site for teens who have questions about homosexuality: www.livehope.org. Remember: No matter what choices you've made or how much you struggle, you are God's son. His grace and forgiveness are always there for you. Because homosexuality is a choice your Creator doesn't want you to make, He will help you overcome it—even during those moments when Satan tries to trip you up. Tell Him everything you're feeling and ask for His guidance.

• **PRAY IT OUT: "Lord, cleanse my heart, heal my sexuality, and help me to grow into the kind of man You created me to be."** If you have doubts about your sexuality, take those fears to Jesus. Ask Him to protect you from Satan's deadly schemes. Ask Jesus to bring solid Christian men into your life who will help guide you into authentic masculinity.

▶▶▶ CONSIDER TAKING TO HEART THIS PRAYER FROM SAINT AUGUSTINE:

> _Almighty God, in whom we live and move and have our being, who hast made us for thyself so that our hearts are restless till they rest in thee: Grant us purity of heart and strength of purpose, that no selfish passion may hinder us from knowing thy will, no weakness from doing it; but that in thy light we may see light clearly, and in thy service find perfect freedom; through Jesus Christ our Lord._

TRIBAL MARKS

A KEY POINT I LEARNED TODAY:

_____

_____

_____

_____

_____

_____

HOW I WANT TO GROW:

_____

_____

_____

_____

_____

MY PRAYER LIST:

_____

_____

_____

_____

_____

_____

SURVIVOR SECRETS

▶ ▶ ▶ **WEEKLY MEMORY VERSE**: *Don't let anyone look down on you because you are young, but set an example for the believers in speech, in life, in love, in faith and in purity.* **—1 Timothy 4:12**

TRIBAL QUEST

Understand that virginity is a precious gift you can give away only once, to the right person, at the right time. Make that gift count.

EXPLORE THE WORD: **Song of Songs 2:1-17**

TRIBAL TRUTH

Marriage is honourable in all, and the bed undefiled. **—Hebrews 13:4, KJV**

TRIBAL FACE

The Most Precious Gift—A Love Story

Kathy walks down the aisle, a train of white silk flowing behind her. White gloves hemmed with silver sequins hold a brilliant bouquet. As Kathy considers the many colors in her hands, she can focus only on one.

White. Pure. Unsoiled. Sinless.

The significance of the color does not escape her. Kathy is grateful—so hugely grateful—she's not living a lie, especially on this day. "Thank You, Jesus," her lips whisper.

Hundreds of people smile as she takes each measured step. Cameras flash, eyes glitter. But Kathy's eyes shine in one direction, for one person alone.

He stands at the end of the aisle, his smile a little nervous, his tie a tad crooked.

He has lots of imperfections. Too crazy about baseball. A little tight with the money. A homeboy who still hasn't learned to make his bed.

But Kathy doesn't care. He has some wonderful strengths, too.

He's transparent and sincere—no need to guess what he's feeling. He's also a hard worker—as long as it doesn't mean making his bed. And he loves Jesus— he can't talk enough about Him.

She knows about the time he was offered a "freebie" by a hooker on the streets of London during that crazy trip to Europe. Kathy smiles, remembering how his face had flushed when he'd finally agreed to tell the story.

"I'd gotten lost," he'd explained. "Separated from my friends, wandering the streets, trying to find the bus station. All I saw was a lady in a pink leather jacket, so I asked her for directions. Then without warning, she flashed her jacket wide open and said, 'How about right here?'

"My mouth fell open, and I sort of stumbled back off the sidewalk. I said, "Uh, no thanks. I just need to find my friends. We hoped to see Big Ben before we go to France. Have you ever been to France? My mom has." Then I spun around and chugged up the street."

Kathy adores her goofy guy.

He's a virgin, just like her. And of all the wedding gifts she just saw in the church foyer, none is so precious as the one he will give her later today.

His purity. His integrity. His masculinity. His patience. His love.

The long walk down the aisle is finally done. He clasps her hand, his smile now beaming, the nervousness gone.

With his touch, Kathy shivers in secret delight. Those hands he's saved for her. His gift—so pure and sweet.

My soon-to-be husband, my first, my only, as I am to him. What a wonderful, blessed, gigantic day.

I'm so glad—so forever glad—we've both waited for it.

Sex has been so abused, so twisted, so commercialized, many Christians have a lurking sense of guilt for even contemplating the subject, even within the God-given boundaries of marriage.

The truth of the matter is that God created sex, and everything He creates is good. The marriage bed truly is undefiled in His eyes. It's so pure, God gave us an entire book of the Bible to describe the wonders of marital intimacy—"The Song of Songs."

Before mankind's fall into sin, "the man and his wife were both naked, and they felt no shame" (Genesis 2:25). It's only because of sin that something pure, something good, seems shameful.

Read this five times slowly: *Sex within marriage is to be enjoyed with loving, mutual abandon.* Lovemaking within the boundaries of a married relationship knows no shame. It's holy. Sex is holy.

The real shame lies in losing your virginity before that special keep-marriage-holy day comes. Why? For starters, think of all the unwanted memories on your wedding night, images attacking your mind like so many harpies.

Is she as hot as the other one was? Is she is as good?

Gag. Spit. Vomit. That skunk will stink up your honeymoon, guaranteed. You want that?

Even if you throw away your virginity on the girl you eventually marry, there will be a lurking guilt, a sickening sense that sex has no boundaries—at least none that you've ever observed. She'll have that same sense. You know what that spells?

Susceptibility.

The unspoken reality is that temptation haunts those who've compromised their purity far more frequently and ferociously than those who have kept it. Statistics show couples who've slept together prior to their wedding are more prone to adultery and divorce. Conversely, virgins who marry virgins are far more likely to have stable marriages.

You cannot mock God on this issue. You sow the seeds of impurity, you will reap a mountain of weeds that will threaten to choke out the real joy of the marriage bed.

But the reverse is also true. You plant the seed of purity, care for it, water it, watch it grow, then one day give the fruit of it to one special woman. You know what? You will reap a sex life that Hollywood can't even imagine, a love that deeply connects souls and not just bodies, a love God totally wants you to thrill in.

A love you desperately want to achieve.

TRIBAL TRAINING

• **Make a goal of reading the entire book of the Song of Songs.** Get a sense of just how special, how intimate, how pure, how thrilling the marriage bed was meant to be.

• **Write out your desire to stay a virgin in the form of a contract to yourself and to God.** List all of the reasons you can imagine for why you want to maintain your purity. Then purpose to give the contract to your future wife on your wedding night.

• **Find healing for past mistakes.** If your virginity is already a thing of the past, you have a lot of heart searching ahead of you. Your virginity cannot be recovered, but a broken, humble spirit before God can do much to heal yesterday's harmful choices. Do a long Bible study on Christ's forgiveness. Follow that with another huge study on the word *purity* and all the words related to it. A concordance will help you with this. God's Word is like water; it can purify stained memories.

• **PRAY IT OUT: "Lord, help me save sex for marriage."** Tell Jesus that you respect the institution of marriage. Ask Him to help you prepare for your future wife by molding you into a disciplined young man; one who respects women and who is committed to purity.

TRIBAL MARKS

A KEY POINT I LEARNED TODAY:

_____

_____

_____

_____

_____

_____

HOW I WANT TO GROW:

_____

_____

_____

_____

_____

_____

MY PRAYER LIST:

_____

_____

_____

_____

_____

_____

A WARRIOR'S BATTLES

PURE ADVENTURE

WEEK 2 ▶▶▶

SURVIVOR SECRETS

▶▶▶**WEEKLY MEMORY VERSE**: *Create in me a pure heart, O God, and renew a steadfast spirit within me. Do not cast me from your presence or take your Holy Spirit from me. Restore to me the joy of your salvation and grant me a willing spirit, to sustain me.* **—Psalm 51:10-12**

TRIBAL QUEST

What a man allows to occupy his mind will eventually determine his actions. Unplug impurity from your life, and strive to nurture a wholesome thought pattern. This is the key to moral and spiritual excellence.

EXPLORE THE WORD: **Philippians 4:4-9**

TRIBAL TRUTH

Finally, brothers, whatever is true, whatever is noble, whatever is right, whatever is pure, whatever is lovely, whatever is admirable—if anything is excellent or praiseworthy—think about such things. **—Philippians 4:8**

PUNCHED OUT BY PORN—TWO STORIES

TRIBAL FACE

Mike, 16
Columbus, Ohio
Caught in the Act

Throughout the past few years, I've looked at porn on the Internet every now and then.

Deep down, I knew it was wrong, but I always found a way to make myself feel okay about it. I'd tell myself stuff like, *Hey, I don't look at it all the time, so it's not a problem,* or, *At least I'm not addicted to it like some people are.*

I thought I was fine because I didn't have a stash under my bed or in my closet. I was a good Christian kid who'd sneak a peek every once in a while. I bet lots of guys can relate.

One day, I decided it was over. I was never going to do it again. A few weeks went by, then I slipped up again. *What's going on inside me?* I wondered.

I thought I had buried my past, yet I couldn't seem to get over this stuff. It was as if I was caught in an invisible porn web—with no way of escape.

Then everything came to a head.

My older sister confronted me, explaining that my younger sister and her friends pulled up the history file on our computer, revealing my past Internet use, a past that I thought I'd erased for good. (I still have no idea how they were able to pull it up, because I did my best to delete everything when I'd determined to change.)

Today, I feel like an idiot for putting my sisters through that. The thought of them trying to explain why those sites were on our computer is so embarrassing. The hardest part is the trust I ruined with my family.

I'm now filled with feelings of sorrow, guilt, and remorse. The entire time I looked at porn, I always thought I had gotten away with it. Yet whether or not other people ever find out, God knows.

So, if you think you've gotten away with your secret, understand this: You're just fooling yourself. What's more, you're attempting to deceive the very people who could be able to help you.

TRIBAL FACE

Kyle, 15
Colorado Springs, Colorado

When I was 12, I discovered the magnificent technological wonder known as the Internet. I enjoyed playing online games and watching short animated films known as "flash movies." One day, when I was browsing a new Web site, something unexpected appeared. I suddenly found myself looking at young women engaged in sexual acts. The only thing was, they were *animated*.

I later found out I'd stumbled into something known as *hentai* (Japanese animated pornography). It offered the same sexual arousal as regular porn, but because it was animated, it showed things that couldn't happen in real life: women being raped by alien life forms, for example. Soon enough, my older sister discovered that I'd been looking at this, and it disgusted her. She threatened to tell our parents if I didn't stop. So, I left the site—for a while.

Unfortunately, I had become as addicted to it as a smoker is to nicotine. My sister ended up telling our parents. They wanted to know how I'd gotten into it. I had lost a great deal of their trust. My dad took away my Internet privileges until we'd gone through a Bible study together on purity. He wanted me to replace all those sinful images with God's truth on sexuality and the right way to look at women—as sisters in Christ, not sex objects. I'm glad my sister told on me. With God's help, I know I can be cured of this addiction.

I'm convinced that the Enemy is working overtime, attempting to catch your eyes with pornography, enslave your heart—and, ultimately, drive your focus away from God.

And to be honest, I'm angry. I'm angered by a multibillion-dollar porn industry that's invading the Internet and the media like a cancer, a business that profits off the addictions of its users. I'm angered by the sickening fact that countless young men are being led down a path to destruction.

But I'm also proud. I'm proud of all the teen guys I've met who have the courage to admit that porn is a problem—and who desire a way out. That's the first step in the right direction.

The question is, what's the next step—and the step after that? How can you stop porn from becoming a pattern, a habit, an addiction—a cancer that destroys your faith? Today's lesson (and Week 3: Seven Strategies for Conquering Lust and Porn) offers some steps that will help get you back on a righteous path.

TRIBAL TRAINING

• **STEP 1: Know that you're not alone!** The silence of sexual struggles has pushed too many Christian guys over the edge. They end up keeping quiet about their "deepest, darkest sins" because they buy a lie: "If I say something, I'll be condemned by everyone—my church, my parents, even God." And a second lie: "I'm the only one who knows about this, so it really doesn't affect anyone else." But get this: You're not alone in your failures—and you don't have to be alone in your healing.

• **STEP 2: Don't fool yourself—you'll eventually get caught.** So, when you find yourself drawn to an immoral act, such as looking at porn—or anything else that would cause you to keep it secret from others—don't do it. Instead, stop, consider the consequences, and pray. Jesus will intervene. Never believe the lie that you can ever say something, do something, go somewhere, or think something that God—and possibly others—won't know about. People who believe in secrets are people who get into trouble. (For more on these topics, see Luke 12:2-3; 1 Corinthians 10:13; and read the lesson in Day 15.)

• **STEP 3: Don't fool yourself—pornography is addicting.** Here's what happens inside your brain:

The visual stimulation of pornography triggers a sexual response (from adrenaline and testosterone) that's more addicting than heroin or cocaine. The overall effect is very much like post-traumatic stress syndrome, just as the smell of diesel fuel can trigger vivid war trauma. Likewise, a young boy who views porn can see and feel the same response to a short skirt, for example, as he did to the initial animation or photo.

The material burns itself into the repetitive porn user's brain. Each time the sexual material is revisited, your body takes a bigger hit.

God sets up barriers to protect us; but each time a barrier is jumped, you get closer to the fire. If you suspect you have an addiction to porn, seek help immediately.[1]

• **STEP 4: Know that God forgives you.** Chances are, you've tried to hide this sin for a long time. Maybe you've confessed it to God, yet are still entangled in guilt—flogging yourself for your mistakes. Understand this: If you've confessed this sin to Jesus Christ, you really are forgiven by God. He knows your deepest secrets and sins—and He loves you in spite of them! You're not condemned for what you've done, and Jesus doesn't hold it against you. If you let Him, God will help you overcome this struggle.

• **STEP 5: Work through the shame.** Shame is guilt run out of control. It's what the devil uses to tell us that, because of whatever we have done, we're bad, worthless, and beyond God's love and forgiveness. You've got to work through these feelings and grasp the truth of God: Regardless of what you've looked at, how many times, with whom, or where, you can start over. While there may be some pain and tough consequences to work through, you can have a new beginning with Christ. He wants to restore your purity. (See Day 16 for more on this subject.)

• **STEP 6: Talk it out.** This is certainly the hardest step of all, but one I encourage you to take: Share your struggle with your parents, your youth pastor, or some other trustworthy Christian adult. Don't bear this alone. Get some help working through the shame. Find someone who can help you maintain a righteous walk.

• **STEP 7: Be willing to run.** Paul told Timothy to "flee also youthful lusts" (2 Timothy 2:22, KJV). I think, basically, he was saying, "Get out while the gettin's good." The longer you play with fire, the more apt you are to get burned. A guy who is serious about directing his drives and staying "porn-free" will take these additional steps:

Cut off the source. Many filtering software packages block sexually explicit material before it comes up on your screen. Install one of these programs.

Don't surf alone. Stay off the Web when you're home alone. Secrecy only adds to the temptation.

Keep the computer out of your bedroom. Put it in a common area, like the kitchen or den, where you know a family member could walk by at any minute.

Let others browse through the history files. What have you got to hide?

Don't use the computer after the rest of your family is in bed. Just like city streets, the Internet (especially chat rooms) becomes more hazardous when traversed in the dark.

• **PRAY IT OUT: "Lord, unplug pornography from my life and help me to steer clear of impurity."** Ask God to cleanse your mind from past mistakes. Ask Him to heal your sexuality and show you how to honor Him with this part of your life.

TRIBAL MARKS

A KEY POINT I LEARNED TODAY:

_____

_____

_____

_____

_____

HOW I WANT TO GROW:

_____

_____

_____

_____

_____

MY PRAYER LIST:

_____

_____

_____

_____

_____

SURVIVOR SECRETS

▶ ▶ ▶ **WEEKLY MEMORY VERSE**: *Create in me a pure heart, O God, and renew a steadfast spirit within me. Do not cast me from your presence or take your Holy Spirit from me. Restore to me the joy of your salvation and grant me a willing spirit, to sustain me.* —**Psalm 51:10-12**

TRIBAL QUEST

When it comes to matters of the heart, learn to separate the lies from the truth.

EXPLORE THE WORD: **2 Peter 2:1-12**

TRIBAL TRUTH

These are rebellious people, deceitful children, children unwilling to listen to the LORD's instruction. —**Isaiah 30:9**

TRIBAL FACE

Charlie and Sarah: When Opposites Don't Attract

One minute, I'm surfing the tube—looking for something decent to watch—and the next minute, I'm outraged. *What I'm seeing can't be real!* I tell myself. *It's got to be staged. But why? Who actually lives this way?*

I've stumbled upon a popular daytime talk show often viewed by young people. Today's topic: "Transvestite Gay Males and Their Female Lovers."

The host is interviewing a homosexual young man named Charlie, who is dressed like a woman, and a lady named Sarah, who is dressed like a man. Both claim to be lovers. Suddenly, the girl pulls an engagement ring out of her jacket pocket and kneels in front of the guy.

"Charlie, we've been friends through high school," she says, "and you know how I feel about you."

The boy blushes, and the audience cheers.

"I want to spend my life with you," Sarah tells Charlie, offering him the ring. "I want to have your children. That's why I'm asking you to marry me."

The audience roars even louder. Even the host begins to pressure him. "So, what's your answer, Charlie?" the TV personality says. "She obviously loves you.

Are you going to say no to this beautiful young lady?"

"But I'm gay," Charlie responds.

"I don't care," his lover says. "I think we can have a good life together."

After a long pause—the audience still cheering—Charlie looks at the host and says, "Yes, I'll marry her. But only because I love that gorgeous ring!"

As outrageous as this scenario may seem, it underscores the twisted sexual climate you are living in, not to mention today's casual attitudes toward sex, love, and marriage.

True, Charlie and Sarah represent an extreme case, certainly not the norm. (What do you expect from daytime TV, right?) Yet a constant bombardment of mixed-up media messages coupled with bad influences from friends is taking a toll on Christian teens.

"I'm not one of those all-media-is-Satan kind of guys," says popular youth speaker and author Justin Lookadoo. "But in the case of sex and romance, it may be true. Do you know how hard it is to find a DVD, CD, or magazine without a bunch of skin-flashin' and sex-talkin'? It's like, that's all there is."[2]

CCM artist Josh Brown, lead singer for Day of Fire, agrees. "Today's young men are drowning in twisted sexual content from movies, TV, music, and the Internet," he says. "It's warping their view of love and relationships. I know this from experience: I came out of the secular music world, and I'm a guy. I've been there, and I see it happening to teen boys everywhere."

When it comes to matters of the heart, too many churched boys are compromising biblical values and caving in to popular culture. Take a look at what's being echoed by teen guys coast to coast:

> **Robert, 15, Durham, North Carolina:** "Sometimes 'hooking up' with the opposite sex is just about fun and recreation, not romance. My girlfriend and I really like each other, and it has come to the point where she and I want to kiss and stuff. But some of my friends say it's wrong in God's eyes to make out. To us, it's not a big deal."

> **Alex, 17, Augusta, Georgia:** "If two unmarried people are having sex in a committed relationship, what should stop them? As a Christian, I've always been taught that premarital sex is wrong,

but the problem is, I can't find Scripture that says this specifically. Why do Christians have to create so many rules for something that everybody is doing?"

Josh, 16, Silverton, Oregon: "I met a girl at camp who has all the qualities I'm looking for—including a strong faith in God. Even though we only spent a week together, I'm convinced that I've found my soul mate. But my parents believe otherwise. They say we're way too young to get serious romantically, especially to think about marriage. Our feelings are real, so what makes us too immature?"

Loose dating morals, confusion about sex and relationships, relying upon emotions instead of biblical guidelines—the list goes on and on. So, how do you rate on the "truth-about-romantic-love scale"?

Let's face it: Next to committing your life to Jesus Christ, setting godly standards for relationships and choosing the path of purity are some of the hardest decisions you will ever make. So, before you even think about dating, examine your motives. Take an honest look at how you view females and relationships. Does your view of women come from God or from the world?

"As a teen, I made many mistakes as I dated," says Josh (from the group Day of Fire). "I've seen how immorality can destroy relationships and cause emotional, physical, and spiritual damage. Here's what I've learned: For any relationship to be successful, Jesus must be first."

TRIBAL TRAINING

• **Learn to navigate sexual landmines.** There's no way around it. We live in a "sex sells" society. Musicians sing about it. Many schools teach that everything is fine as long as you wear a condom. It's a tough time to be a guy who's trying to stay pure, but you can make it. There's hope. (Hey, you're reading this book!) You can guard your heart from major attack by separating the lies from the truth.

Popular Media Say:

Everybody's doing it.
Having sex makes you a man.
Sex proves love.

Controlling it is dangerous; you have to let it out.

Sex is a game; score as much as you can.

You can keep it casual.

A condom will keep you safe.

When she says no, she really means yes.

Youth is the time for good, wild sex.

Virginity is for doofuses.

God Says:

Those who trust Me aren't doing it.

A real man can control his urges.

Real love wants My best for her.

Sexual passion is strong, but My love is stronger.

Marriage is the only "safe sex."

There is no such thing as "casual sex."

Condoms are worthless against emotional scars.

No means no. Her body is not her own—and it's certainly not yours.

There's a reason all your studies show that a good marriage equals good sex.

I created animals to procreate. But humans can be happy only by reflecting Me.

• **Follow God's design for love and romance.** Love. It's probably the most overused word in the English language. You might say: "I love Dad and Mom," "I love pepperoni pizza," "I love God." Love means something different in each case.

In the Bible, the word *love* often refers to action—something we do rather than something we feel. John 3:16 says, "God so loved the world that he gave. . . ." This verse refers to love as an action; something that God did for us. In other places throughout Scripture, love is defined as selfless giving to others, of manifesting attitudes of kindness, patience, humility, and commitment in relationships.

Love for your lady goes way beyond simple emotions. It involves commitment.

It means putting her needs above your own: "It is not rude, it is not self-seeking, it is not easily angered, it keeps no record of wrongs. Love does not delight in evil but rejoices with the truth" (1 Corinthians 13:5-6).

• **PRAY IT OUT: "Lord, protect me from the lies and myths about love and romance."** Ask Jesus to help you walk in the truth—never veering from a path to purity.

A KEY POINT I LEARNED TODAY:

_____

_____

_____

_____

_____

_____

HOW I WANT TO GROW:

_____

_____

_____

_____

_____

_____

MY PRAYER LIST:

_____

_____

_____

_____

_____

_____

_____

SURVIVOR SECRETS

▶▶▶ **WEEKLY MEMORY VERSE**: *Create in me a pure heart, O God, and renew a steadfast spirit within me. Do not cast me from your presence or take your Holy Spirit from me. Restore to me the joy of your salvation and grant me a willing spirit, to sustain me.* —Psalm 51:10-12

TRIBAL QUEST

Be the kind of young man who strives to be uncompromising in his attitude toward sexual sin—not one who settles for "technical virginity."

EXPLORE THE WORD: 1 Corinthians 6:18-21

TRIBAL TRUTH

Do you not know that your body is a temple of the Holy Spirit, who is in you, whom you have received from God? You are not your own. —1 Corinthians 6:19

CROSSING THE LINE—TWO STORIES

TRIBAL FACE

Tim, 17
Jacksonville, Florida
Case of a Cuddle-Crazed Kid

It's a sticky summer night in Jacksonville, Florida, but Tim isn't complaining. He's reclining on the sun porch of his parents' beach house—with his arms wrapped tightly around the waist of a girl he met a few days earlier.

His folks' long-awaited date night provides the perfect opportunity for some teen romance of his own. And since Tim made a pledge for purity at church, he's convinced that nothing will move beyond kissing—and *cuddling*.

It's not like we're doing anything wrong.

Brian, 16
Grand Rapids, Michigan
A New Twist on Group Dating

The party is in full swing at 16-year-old Brian's house. But instead of screaming teens falling out the windows, the lights are dimmed, and everyone is strangely . . . sedate! This Grand Rapids, Michigan, boy is leading the crowd in a "cuddle game."

The dozen or so friends Brian invited are paired up, guy-girl, and are in "spooning" positions on his living-room floor.

"Okay—switch NOW!" a voice blurts. The room fills with laughter and commotion (more like a party) as each teen scrambles to find another partner.

"Freeze!" someone shouts, and Brian's house becomes quiet again. Everywhere, bodies are locked together in tight embraces.

The rules:

1. Keep your clothes on.
2. No touching in private places.

Spooning, cuddling—regardless of what teens are calling it, the activity has become an accepted way for some to get close "without getting hurt," they claim. Even a number of Christian youth are becoming cuddle-crazed. Take a look at what a young man from Dallas recently shared with me. (He asked to remain anonymous.)

"I've always believed in keeping my virginity until marriage. However, my current girlfriend has a different viewpoint about sex. In her opinion, it's okay to engage in an intimate activity, as long as that activity does not include the word *sex*. She has a strong faith and is confident in her belief that no sin is committed if 'other playful things are done'—such as kissing, cuddling, and touching. Her thoughts and confidence have created confusion within me. Are her interpretations right or wrong? How do we know where to draw the line?"

Too many guys share this boy's confusion. How about you? If we're honest with ourselves, we have to admit that "playing around sexually" is still *"playing around sexually"*—which means we're treading into dangerous territory.

Sex is progressive. As guys, once our engines are fired up, our "internal-control centers" scream *go!*, not stop. And the further we go, the harder stopping becomes.

Instead of asking, "How far can we go without crossing the line?" just don't compromise at all. Flee from anything that's questionable. Above all, choosing to remain pure isn't a matter of "technical virginity:" "Hey, at least we didn't have intercourse, so it's not really sin." Yeah, right.

I like what a friend of mine once said: "God's concern for virginity is not a matter of anatomy but of privacy. He wants us to reserve our 'private parts' for the privacy of marriage."

TRIBAL TRAINING

• **Don't kid yourself with "everything but intercourse is okay."** As harmless as spooning and cuddling may seem, even the act of lying down with a girl is intimate. As I mentioned above, sexual activity is progressive—beginning with a simple glance and moving through increasing levels of touch. With each step comes a greater degree of risk.

• **Know where Christians draw the line.** Flip through the Bible, and you'll uncover the standards God wants us to follow: look at 1 Corinthians 6:18, Ephesians 5:3, Hebrews 13:4.

• **Always check your motives.** Before you find yourself in a compromising situation with a girl, decide your response now. And when in doubt, ask yourself three questions:

1. What is the motivation of my heart?
2. Am I showing respect for the opposite sex?
3. Will this lead me to "out-of-control" behavior?

• **PRAY IT OUT: "Lord, help me to avoid seeing how far I can go without crossing the line sexually."** Ask the Lord to give you the strength to be a real man of God—one who seeks to be uncompromising in his attitude toward sin.

TRIBAL MARKS

A KEY POINT I LEARNED TODAY:

HOW I WANT TO GROW:

MY PRAYER LIST:

SURVIVOR SECRETS

▶ ▶ ▶ **WEEKLY MEMORY VERSE**: *Create in me a pure heart, O God, and renew a steadfast spirit within me. Do not cast me from your presence or take your Holy Spirit from me. Restore to me the joy of your salvation and grant me a willing spirit, to sustain me.* **—Psalm 51:10-12**

TRIBAL QUEST

Learning to treat the opposite sex with respect—seeing girls as people, not as a nice set of curves—will help keep "sex" out of your mind.

EXPLORE THE WORD: **Genesis 29:1-21**

TRIBAL TRUTH

Do not rebuke an older man harshly, but exhort him as if he were your father. Treat younger men as brothers, older women as mothers, and younger women as sisters, with absolute purity. **—1 Timothy 5:1-2**

TRIBAL FACE

Jacob
A Home Full of Headaches

In the Bible, there's the story of a man who eventually ended up with four wives, 13 kids, and a home full of headaches. The guy's name was Jacob.

Having more than one wife at a time is definitely outside of God's design. There was only one Eve for Adam, something Jacob should have known. Not paying attention to that little detail cost him big-time.

For starters, Jacob's daughter, Dinah, got raped, and her brothers wiped out an entire town in revenge. Then the oldest son, Reuben, slept with his mother's servant, Bilhah, one of Jacob's four wives. Eventually, another of Jacob's sons, Judah, went to bed with his own daughter-in-law—thinking she was a prostitute—and left her pregnant with twins.

What a reeking mess.

Ever notice how *honest* the Bible is on the subject of sex? No attempt at cover-ups. That's good.

Jacob's walk with God, like so many of our own, was a mixed bag of holy hopes and crass carnality. It didn't have to be that way, but that's the way it was.

As a young man, Jacob was a model of patience and purity for seven long years. The beautiful Rachel caught his eye; "love at first sight" perfectly describes it. The fact that Jacob got to kiss her the first day they met doesn't necessarily imply impurity. Jacob ended up getting kissed by her father, Laban, that day, too. In that culture, they said, "Hello, how are you?" with a smooch.

What's significant is that Jacob cried his eyes out after kissing Rachel. That's not hormones in overdrive. That's deep, genuine, heart-wrenching love.

And what was Jacob willing to do to win Rachel's hand? Seven years of slave labor for a conniving cheat who would one day be his father-in-law. It's tough to understand Jacob's thinking in this story: *He* was the one who chose the seven years, not Laban. Most of us probably would have offered seven days. Perhaps Jacob knew that the hard-driving Laban would be nowhere near satisfied with less.

But maybe it was Jacob's way of saying to Rachel, "You're worth seven years of my life." For seven long, laborious years, Jacob proved his love for Rachel.

And during all that time, he was an absolute gentleman. In other words, he didn't sleep with the girl of his dreams.

Speaking of which, let's look at something that hardly anyone has the guts to talk about: wet dreams. You can bet that some of Jacob's dreams about Rachel during those seven years were exactly that: wet.

Wet dreams are God's gift to you as a single guy to ease your sexual tension. Physically, your body needs to relieve its ongoing production of semen. Emotionally, you also need a release, because sex is such a driving force in your makeup as a man. Wet dreams are not dirty; they're not sinful. Every time you experience one, you can thank God you've enjoyed another month or so of sexual purity. Ask Him for the grace to be pure again for the next month and then go back to sleep. You're a man who's learning to control his sexual desires.

You're a man who's come a long way in treating girls as people, not as eye-candy for selfish gratification. Girls instinctively know when a guy looks at them with respect. So, what does treating girls with respect look like? Keep reading!

TRIBAL TRAINING

• **Raise the bar on the use of sexual innuendo.** Sex can be discussed openly, in a way that honors God, in a way that pushes us to greater purity. We trust this book is a good example of that. But sex can also be discussed in a dishonoring, trashy way. We all know where that line is, but we love to play with it via innuendo—disguised references to a taboo subject. It's especially exciting when girls are around to hear our clever bedroom humor. That needs to stop.

• **Never make fun of a girl's looks.** That kind of joke hurts to the core, in a way we guys have a hard time understanding. Make enough of them, and you may condemn yourself to a life of bachelorhood. Moreover, the choice of joke material says more about the joker than it does about the joke's victim. Humor tends to reflect the fixations of a person's mind. If all you can joke about is a girl's body, you had better ask yourself where your thoughts are traveling.

• **Enough with the potty talk.** References to bodily functions, noises, and smells are not always wrong, but some guys talk as if they live in an outhouse. A few girls will laugh, but most are looking for someone less juvenile.

• **Forget bragging; ask girls questions about their lives.** A guy who can't help talking about himself around girls is a self-serving jerk. He's merely out to impress, and his core motive is to use. Any girl who falls for such a guy is a flake. Inevitably, she'll come out of the relationship disillusioned, empty, wondering why this guy never cared about her as much as she did him. A true gentleman impresses girls by accident, through a genuine interest in their lives. And that sincerity will carry itself into a healthy marriage relationship.

• **Keep confidences under verbal lock and key.** If a girl confides in you and finds out the next day that she was yesterday's lunchroom dialogue, you deserve to be dead meat. She's trusted you with something near and dear. Respect knows how to keep that trust.

• **Give up on the groping.** Some guys will touch a woman for any reason, often in the guise of horseplay or as a form of greeting. Co-ed football and friendly hugs are fine as long as your motives are pure (2 Corinthians 13:12). If something dark lurks in your heart, however, back off.

• **Concentrate on inner beauty.** If your hormones always have you hovering around the hottest-looking girls—to the exclusion of all others—you don't have a clue about inner beauty. This isn't about marrying an ugly girl with a nice personality. This is about relating sincerely to any girl, outwardly beautiful or otherwise. This is also about avoiding a life sentence with a gorgeous girl who's got the heart of a snake.

• **Memorize 1 Timothy 5:1-2.** Your sisters in Christ need the "absolute purity" this verse speaks of—from you, their brother. The guys of this world sure aren't going to give it to them. You can.

• **PRAY IT OUT: "Lord, help me to respect the opposite sex."** Ask God to give you new vision—a new, pure way of looking at women.

TRIBAL MARKS

A KEY POINT I LEARNED TODAY:

_____

_____

_____

_____

_____

_____

HOW I WANT TO GROW:

_____

_____

_____

_____

_____

_____

MY PRAYER LIST:

_____

_____

_____

_____

_____

_____

_____

SURVIVOR SECRETS

▶▶▶ **WEEKLY MEMORY VERSE**: *Create in me a pure heart, O God, and renew a steadfast spirit within me. Do not cast me from your presence or take your Holy Spirit from me. Restore to me the joy of your salvation and grant me a willing spirit, to sustain me.* —**Psalm 51:10-12**

TRIBAL QUEST

Your virginity is a precious gift you can give away only once, to the right woman, at the right time—marriage. So learn a secret from young Joseph in the Bible: Save yourself for God's best.

EXPLORE THE WORD: **Genesis 39**

TRIBAL TRUTH

Be self-controlled and alert. Your enemy the devil prowls around like a roaring lion looking for someone to devour. Resist him, standing firm in the faith, because you know that your brothers throughout the world are undergoing the same kind of sufferings. —**1 Peter 5:8-9**

TRIBAL FACE

Michael's Journey
Waiting Is Worth It

What if I never meet the right girl?

What if I turn out to be a failure with the opposite sex?

What if I'm destined to spend my whole life alone?

What if . . .

The questions swarmed my brain like an army of bloodthirsty mosquitoes, and then waged a war on the pit of my stomach. I was 15 and had just been slammed hard by a very painful, very lonely, avoid-at-any-cost experience: *rejection*.

My buddy, Alan, had the brilliant idea of setting me up with one of our school's most popular eighth-graders.

"Sheila?!" I gasped. "Are you crazy? We say hi in the halls, and she signed my

yearbook last year—but she's not interested in me."

"I'm positive she likes you," Alan insisted. "I'm never wrong about these things."

Mistake Number. 1: Never listen to a guy who claims he's never wrong about girls.

After pointing me in her direction, he smiled. "She's alone . . . waiting for you to make a move," he said. "Now stop being a wimp and get yourself a girlfriend."

Mistake Number 2: Never believe that being "girl-less" means being a wimp.

I swallowed back my fear and inched my way toward Sheila. Being a wimp started to seem a lot easier—especially if I could melt into a crack on the floor.

Mistake Number 3: Never try to force a casual friendship into something romantic without learning more about her first.

Sheila flashed her unforgettable smile—the one that always turned up the speed on my heart.

I cleared my throat and felt my mind go immediately blank: "I was thinking . . . Well, Alan told me . . . What I'm trying to say is, I like you, and it would be cool if . . ."

Before I could pry loose another word from my tongue, Sheila's warm expression had turned into a cold stare. And without saying a word, she walked right past me and practically decked Alan. "If Michael asks," she snarled, "you're *dead!*" She quickly disappeared into the girls' restroom.

Alan looked at me with a sheepish grin. "Ouch!" he said.

The last thing I remember was melting into a crack in the floor.

I survived my first big female flop and eventually learned the basics of impressing a girl—like . . . *never* stepping on cracks when I'm feeling wimpy and *always* striving to find complete sentences when attempting to communicate.

But as I grew into masculinity, I discovered a frustrating fact about us guys: Regardless of our age or how much we've dated, we'd rather be flogged, quartered, and burned at the stake than risk rejection from the opposite sex.

I was never more aware of this than when I knelt in front of the woman I deeply love—Tiffany Cox—and asked the ultimate question: "Will you marry me?"

It was Christmas Eve 1996, and Tiffany and I had spent the afternoon hiking in the wilderness near her parents' home in Pineville, West Virginia.

"This is my favorite spot," Tiffany said when we reached the end of the trail—a steep ridge with a postcard-perfect view. "I used to come here when I had big decisions to pray about."

"I can see why," I said. "This place definitely feels closer to God."

Rugged mountains and misty groves of oak and spruce stretched endlessly across the West Virginia landscape. It didn't take a bolt of lightning (or my buddy, Alan) to convince me that the setting was ideal and the moment was *right*. More important, I knew that Tiffany was the *right* woman.

Asking this incredible lady to spend her life with me involved a risk. After all, God could have had other plans for Tiffany. Yet several key things had given me confidence:

Tiffany and I had built our relationship on a foundation of . . .

Faith. Jesus' will for our lives was the center of our desires. He defined our self-worth, not the status of having someone to date.

Friendship. We'd spent a little more than two years getting to know each other. This meant countless hours of fun together and asking questions, some of them deep and difficult. True intimacy always grows slowly out of the solid soil of "knowing" each other casually and intently.

Support. We kept our relationship within sight of our families. One of the first steps I took was to ask Tiffany's dad for his permission to get married, as well as his blessing on our life together.

Purity. Nothing gives me more pride than being able to admit that we made a commitment to stay pure for each other—and for God.

I reached into my jacket pocket and pulled out a small velvet box, then handed it to Tiffany. "I have an early Christmas gift for you," I said.

She ran her finger across the lid and smiled. "I bet it's jewelry!"

As Tiffany reached in and gently pulled out a diamond engagement ring, the expression on her face gave me a solid clue to her answer.

Far from a cold stare, she was beaming.

I quickly knelt. "I couldn't imagine spending the rest of this life without you," I said. "Will you marry me?"

Tiffany's smile grew even bigger. "Yes!"

Before we headed down the mountain to share the news with Tiffany's family,

I spent some time talking to my Father: "Thank You, God, for this priceless woman You've given me. Waiting for her has been worth it. I give You this marriage. Bless it, use it, and let Your will be done."

Your engagement may be several years down the road. But your dream of one day spending your life with the right woman is a dream to take seriously. Don't set yourself up for a fall by forcing romantic expectations on every girl on whom you get a crush. Instead, build a firm foundation for your future marriage by making a commitment to seeking God's will and saving yourself for His best.

And as you grow into masculinity—and closer to finding the woman of your dreams—never forget: Waiting is worth it!

TRIBAL TRAINING

• **If dating is in your future, realize that behind every pretty face is a person with feelings.** The girl you date today will eventually be someone's wife. Whether yours or someone else's, man, you are the leader. You need to give her respect, not baggage. Selfishness is a monster that destroys relationships. It's your responsibility to protect her.

• **Consider "non-dating."** I can hear you asking, *Huh?* Because dating is a high-pressure, one-on-one situation, accompanied by expectations, sweaty palms, lumps in the throat, and bungled intentions, non-dates can be a nice alternative. Non-dates take the pressure off: a group setting, less formal, no possibility of "getting somewhere." In other words, a better chance to *be yourself.*

It's easier to get to know someone on a non-date. It's also easier to ask someone out on a non-date. For instance:

The typical date pick-up line: "Hey, Sara, would you . . . uh . . . I mean . . . uh . . . how about you and me . . . uh . . . "

Smooth, right?

The non-date alternative: "Hey, Sara, a bunch of us are getting together for some volleyball at the park this Saturday. Want to come?"

If she turns you down—it's no big deal, because you weren't asking her out on a *date*. And you can walk away with your self-esteem intact.[3]

• **Never pursue a non-Christian.** Take a look at 2 Corinthians 6:14-15. It says,

"Do not be yoked together with unbelievers. For what do righteousness and wickedness have in common? Or what fellowship can light have with darkness? . . . What does a believer have in common with an unbeliever?" These are good questions to ask yourself.

The fact is, when two people are yoked together, they must both pull in the same direction in order to make any progress at all. But by definition, Christians and non-Christians are headed in different directions. Apply this to romance, and you've got disaster. (The couple ends up going nowhere, and they keep rubbing sores on each other in the process.) Getting involved romantically just won't work. Find a mate who says "God" a lot, but knows *whom* they're actually talking about.

• **PRAY IT OUT: "Lord, as I relate to the opposite sex, guard my heart and my actions."** Ask God to give you a clear picture of the kind of woman He wants you to marry.

TRIBAL MARKS

A KEY POINT I LEARNED TODAY:

HOW I WANT TO GROW:

MY PRAYER LIST:

DAY 13: MAKING A PACT FOR PURITY

▶▶▶ **WEEKLY MEMORY VERSE**: *Create in me a pure heart, O God, and renew a steadfast spirit within me. Do not cast me from your presence or take your Holy Spirit from me. Restore to me the joy of your salvation and grant me a willing spirit, to sustain me.* —**Psalm 51:10-12**

TRIBAL QUEST

Win the battle against lust by taking up arms, joining forces with other warriors, and making a public pact for purity.

EXPLORE THE WORD: 2 Timothy 2:22-26

TRIBAL TRUTH

Flee the evil desires of youth, and pursue righteousness, faith, love and peace, along with those who call on the Lord out of a pure heart. —**2 Timothy 2:22**

TRIBAL FACE

Seven Colorado Guys Celebrate Purity

It's Friday night, and we're heading to a party. Actually, it's more of a "heaven-bound bash" celebrating purity.

Cruising down a busy parkway, we see a shadowy, X-rated gentleman's club on the right side of a rushing stream of traffic. Merging into the left lane, we ease into the parking lot of a tiny church. It stands almost unnoticed opposite the strip club. We've crossed a literal battle line between lust and virtue.

The church's youth pastor, Rick, has invited everyone in town to a victory party. Teen guys in his ministry are overcoming lust, so his church is celebrating. During the next hour, we'll listen to the stories and struggles of these young men, and we'll learn about their commitment to withstand the Enemy in an area that every young man battles: sexual purity.

Pastor Rick organized tonight's ceremony for seven guys in his discipleship group. The point of this special service is to give these teens a chance to go public with their pact for purity. One by one, with all eyes on them, they'll sign a covenant for purity—an official document the guys thought up themselves. Next, their parents will pray with them, then each will be given a purity ring. In the days ahead, the rings will serve as a reminder of their commitment.

We take a seat in the sanctuary and begin thanking God for this amazing evening—especially for these gutsy young men.

That night represented a true victory in the battle against lust. Seven Christian boys had the courage to stand up in front of their entire church, admit their struggles with lust, and make commitments to purity.

How about you? When it comes to purity, would you be willing to make this kind of public stand? The fact that you're reading this book means that you're fighting the battle—and that you desire victory.

At times you've felt defeated, abandoned by God, and riddled with guilt for your weaknesses. You've probably even listened to the lie Satan whispers in your ear. (*"You're alone in this battle."*) You've probably even thought of giving up altogether and surrendering to the enemy. (*"That's right, you can't fight it."*) Maybe you're barely holding on, praying for one last ounce of hope—desperately hoping something in these pages can help.

Guess what? You found it.

The testimonies of those seven young men—Scott, Bobby, Michael, Nathan, Ricky, Donovan, and Kevin—reveal a path to purity, a journey that started with a realization: They all deal with lust and temptation in some form or another.

Donovan confessed he'd come to a point where he wanted to compromise with temptation. "I was about to do some things that weren't right, and God came to me and said, 'Don't compromise. It's like drinking salt water. [Gratification] will last for a moment, but in the end, it'll only leave you dry and alone.'"

WHERE ARE YOUR WEAK AREAS? The enemy will attack where you're most vulnerable, and the easiest targets are the eyes and ears. Kevin, a high-school junior, openly admits he used to be the one who told the dirty jokes along with friends and even became addicted to pornography in junior high. Hanging out with certain people and watching certain TV shows constantly fed his addiction. "Anytime I was tempted, I'd pray. I just realized that the more I focused on God, [the struggle] wasn't so hard anymore."

DO YOU FIND YOURSELF IN THOSE SHOES? Are you fighting a losing battle against temptation on other fronts? Once you've identified areas of weakness, it's time to begin using the defensive weapons God's given you.

TRIBAL TRAINING

•**Take up your arms, guys: God's Word.** It's the same weapon used by Christ when He was tempted, but how effective is it in defending purity? "With memorizing verses, you can pop that Scripture out right away. It helps if you write it down. It helps us with our thought life and gets rid of the lust. It's just a great thing," says Nathan. Kevin has verses in his wallet and pasted in his gym and hall lockers. He also has some memorized. "So, when I really get down, I can pull out my wallet, I can open up my locker and see that I'm a new creation, that the old has gone, the new has come. I don't have to deal with impurity. I can just focus on God. That's my defense."

You might be saying, "Yeah, yeah, yeah, I've tried that, but it's so easy to slip up!" That leads us to another very important weapon.

• **Find accountability.** Pastor Rick began meeting with the magnificent seven to develop a discipleship group (a.k.a. D-group). The first thing they focused on was their relationship with God. Rick set a goal for the guys to have a devotional time five times each week consisting of worship, Bible reading, and prayer time. Michael describes it as "spending a lot of time with God in His Word and replacing lust with a love for God." Bobby admits that it was hard at first to get into the habit of regular quiet time with God. "I think that brought me closer to Him. I've been able to put down a lot of the lustful things in my life."

The second area of accountability was in sexual temptation. "We hit those issues right away, really hard," Pastor Rick explained. "I took them one at a time and said, 'You can tell me what you are dealing with, and we are going to start praying right now.'" They also started reading *Every Young Man's Battle*, a book that forced the guys to talk openly about sexual issues. Rick admitted the discussion was tough, sometimes shocking, and all-out embarrassing at times. But it's showed these guys how to live in purity.

And what's been the result? How tight do you think this D-group is? On certain occasions they have confronted one another on rebellion issues with parents, as well as bad relationships that could lead down the wrong path. "It's pretty much an open session. We feel pretty safe keeping accountable to each other," Michael says. "There's nothing that we can't say to each other. There's a trust. We don't feel ashamed to tell each other anything," Scott says. How many friends can you say that about?

• **Join this band of brothers: Make a pact for purity.** Each guy's journey made their ceremonial night very significant—a true celebration. Each one had fought long and hard and looked ahead for more battles to be won. Now it's your turn.

—TAKE TO HEART "A WARRIOR'S PURITY CREED" (based on Acts 10:15 and written by Daniel, 16, another Colorado teen who is fighting the battle). Post it by your bed, place it in your Bible, or put it on the inside of your locker—anywhere and everywhere you most need it.

A WARRIOR'S PURITY CREED

I refuse to put myself in situations where I am tempted to compromise my purity.

I commit to the Job Covenant (Job 31:1). I make a covenant with my eye, to keep my mind pure, and not look lustfully at a girl.

I take every thought captive and make it obedient to Christ.

My body is God's temple. I refuse to defile it in any possible way.

I commit to filling my mind and heart with God's Word in order to stay pure (Psalm 119:9).

I commit to having accountability with a few other men of God.

I choose to memorize at least one verse a day that will teach me and train me to be pure and to live a pure life.

I read my commitments to purity every day.

I ask for the Lord's strength and power.

I ask God to keep me from evil and from temptation.

Every time I am tempted, I run to God as fast as I can.

I listen to and read things that encourage me to go after purity.

I don't view purity as a line but a lifestyle. Purity is my purpose and my pursuit. Because of Jesus I am free, and I use my freedom to become more like Christ and have a heart of purity (John 10:10).

—MAKE A TRIBAL PACT FOR PURITY. Ask your mom, dad, or youth pastor to set aside uninterrupted time for a special ceremony of your own. Pick out a cross necklace, a ring, or a watch beforehand and ask your parents to present it to you as a symbol of purity. (Even if you've already done something like this at youth group, it's more powerful if you also have this experience with your dad and/or mom.)

—FIND A MENTOR WITH WHOM YOU CAN TALK OPENLY ABOUT SEXUAL MATTERS. Confess your struggles and find the right Christian guy to answer any and every question you have. Make it someone willing to share the personal struggles he faced growing up. Spend some time praying together. (See Day 19 for more information/suggestions.)

• **PRAY IT OUT: "Lord, give me Your strength to win my battle against lust."** Ask God to cleanse you from past sins. Tell Him you desire a new beginning. Ask Jesus for the daily strength and courage to stay on a path to purity.

TRIBAL MARKS

A KEY POINT I LEARNED TODAY:

_____

_____

_____

_____

_____

_____

HOW I WANT TO GROW:

_____

_____

_____

_____

_____

_____

MY PRAYER LIST:

_____

_____

_____

_____

_____

_____

_____

DAY 14: YOUR FATHER'S BLESSING

▶▶▶ **WEEKLY MEMORY VERSE**: *Create in me a pure heart, O God, and renew a steadfast spirit within me. Do not cast me from your presence or take your Holy Spirit from me. Restore to me the joy of your salvation and grant me a willing spirit, to sustain me.* —**Psalm 51:10-12**

TRIBAL QUEST

Deep inside, sons of all ages share a father hunger: Men yearn to be blessed and affirmed by their earthly dads. Cry out "Abba Father," and experience your heavenly Father's blessing.

EXPLORE THE WORD: **Galatians 3:26-4:7**

TRIBAL TRUTH

Because you are sons, God sent the Spirit of his Son into our hearts, the Spirit who calls out, "Abba, Father." —**Galatians 4:6**

TRIBAL FACE

Keith, 16
Pasadena, California
Starving from Father Hunger

If God really cares, then why have all these bad things happened to me?

If God really cares, then why do I feel so alone?

If God really cares, then why did my father abandon me?

Keith jotted the questions at the top of a sheet of notebook paper—just below the title, "The Worst Year of My Life!"

The stressed-out 16-year-old had made a commitment to Christ at camp a few years back, but lately, he couldn't help wondering if God had given up on him. It was the perfect essay topic for Mrs. Gowler's fifth-period English assignment.

Throughout the year, a ton of bad things had happened to Keith: He'd had two brain tumors, which required surgery and forced doctors to drain fluid from his head; his dad walked out on his mom, little sister, and him; and his family moved across the country.

To top if off, Keith even broke his leg during a youth-group ski trip two weeks previously. He put down his notebook and scowled at the bulky cast on his leg. "Why doesn't God just strike me dead and be done with me?" he asked.

Cindy, his girlfriend—who was busy drawing cartoons on his cast—looked up. "Don't talk that way," she said. "God isn't doing this to you. Times are hard, but He's still with you. And He'll get you through this—if you'll let Him."

Keith looked at her. Despite feeling lousy, he knew Cindy was right. Deep inside, he knew God hadn't left him. And when he thought about it, Christ had often revealed Himself in a loving way—usually through the kind actions of Cindy.

His mind flashed back to his first day of high school after moving from Boston to Southern California. His parents had just divorced, so he and his mom and sister moved to the other side of the country to live near relatives. Keith was confused and bitter. He resented his family's split-up and blamed his mom. And he was angry with his dad for not being a proper father. Suddenly in a strange city, he didn't know anybody. Yet everyone at school seemed to know him.

Keith had a shaved head with a big scar on top. He also used crutches, because his balance was shaky after brain surgery. He looked as though he'd just been through a war—obviously on the losing side. And that's how everyone treated him . . . except Cindy.

Keith sat up on the couch and shifted the pillow under his cast. "So, why do you care so much about a guy like me?" Keith asked.

"Because you're worth caring for," Cindy responded.

"Sure you're not just feeling sorry for a hard-luck case?"

Cindy held the marker in her hand like a dagger and raised it over Keith's chest. "Keep talking that way, and I'll put you out of your misery. If you're a hard-luck case, then so am I."

Keith kissed Cindy's cheek and grinned. He knew she really cared—and understood his pain.

During his first few months in Pasadena, Keith often skipped lunch or would eat in a quiet stairwell at school. He always felt as if everybody was staring at him, so he did everything he could to stay out of sight. And his family's troubles made him too depressed to be social. That's when he ended up meeting Cindy.

She was sitting alone in a stairwell, crying. Keith couldn't resist talking to her.

"I know you," Keith said, leaning on one crutch and cocking his head sideways. "You're in my history class."

Cindy rubbed her eyes, then squinted. "You're Keith, right?"

"Yeah—we both sit in the back of the room."

"Sorry, but I'm kind of a mess right now."

"Mind if I ask what's wrong?"

Cindy wiped another tear from her cheek. "Do you have the rest of the day to listen? It's family stuff, and I'm sure I'd bore you."

"Hey, I'm an expert on family problems," Keith said as he carefully lowered himself to sit down beside her. "In fact, I am a family problem."

Cindy smiled and sniffed. "Well, for starters, everybody fights all the time. And I think my parents are going to get a divorce—"

It was the first of many intense conversations. In the weeks that followed, they formed a close friendship. Now it seemed they'd known each other all their lives.

Cindy put the finishing touches on the cartoons she had drawn on Keith's cast. "Voilá!" she said. "My masterpiece is finished."

Keith looked at the drawings and flashed a fake smile. "Uh, great—what are they?"

"They're cartoons of us," Cindy said, half laughing. "The dark clouds behind are the problems we've had. And this is you and me touching the cross while the sun is shining on us. Cool, huh?"

"Very cool," Keith said as he turned his head and glanced into the kitchen at his mom—where she was hard at work, preparing dinner. "You know. I've been thinking. We're survivors, aren't we?"

"No, we're conquerors," Cindy said. "God has healed you from brain tumors. And He has even brought you and your mom closer together."

Keith locked eyes with Cindy. "He fixed your family, too."

"We're far from fixed," she said. "But at least Mom and Dad have agreed to stay together, and our church is really supporting us. That's a start."

Later that night, Keith scratched out the title on his essay and instead scribbled a new title: Awesome Discovery. Suddenly, the words began to flow. . . .

> After a few years of depression and desperately wishing I could crawl in a hole and die, I met a beautiful girl named Cindy, and she helped to turn on a "light" inside me.
>
> Once I began to understand who Jesus Christ was, it didn't take long for me to trust Him as my Savior—and my "Abba Father."
>
> My family was broken—and so was my heart. Even my body was weak and infected. Yet God didn't give up. He put my life in a cast, so to speak, and began the painful healing process.

When I thought God didn't care, He was right there. When I didn't think I had a purpose in life, as it turns out, I was being molded for work in His kingdom.

Life still isn't easy. I've still got scars. But now I have faith and a rock-solid foundation that no one can tear down. I have God's promise that He will never leave. And because of that, I'm learning to forgive the dad He gave me, the one who's nearly buried himself beneath so many bad decisions.

Do you feel as though your life is in a cast? Are problems at home making you wonder if God really cares about you?

No doubt, Keith experienced more pain than most people endure in a lifetime, yet this teen, along with his girlfriend, made an awesome discovery: Despite the storms we encounter in life, God never leaves us. Even though we are weak, He is able. We can cry out "Abba, Father" and find comfort, strength, and affirmation from Him.

Okay, I know what you're thinking: *What does my father's blessing have to do with my fight for purity?* The answer? Everything.

Whether or not you're willing to admit it, your earthly father has been one of the greatest influences on your life. In fact, there are two critical periods of a young boy's life when he needs a man's influence. From birth to six years of age, a boy "rehearses" his masculinity from his father. Then during the teen years, a boy is released from the nest by his dad. A father instinctively teaches his adolescent son how to launch confidently into masculinity, which includes important stuff like fighting lust and staying on a path to purity.

But if a boy is abandoned by his father, or if Dad is too busy, gone too much, is an alcoholic, or is otherwise caught up in his own problems or his career, the boy can suffer seriously.

Even if you have an imperfect dad—or, like Keith, one who isn't in your life at all—God is your model of a father. There is One who has adopted you and who wants to love you in a way you have never experienced. He will help you in all the battles you face—especially the fight for purity. He will show you what authentic masculinity is all about.

In the next few paragraphs, let's explore ways of mending wounds with your earthly dad—and growing closer to "Abba, Father."

• **Make peace with your earthly dad.** "I love you." "I'm proud of you." "I enjoy watching God mold you into a very special young man." Admit it: These are transforming words, especially when they come from the mouths of our fathers. And even the toughest guy must admit that he longs to receive approval from his dad. Jesus received a verbal stamp of approval from His Father: "As soon as Jesus was baptized, he went up out of the water. At that moment heaven was opened, and he saw the Spirit of God descending like a dove and lighting on him. And a voice from heaven said, 'This is my Son, whom I love; with him I am well pleased'" (Matthew 3:16-17).

So, how do you get a blessing from your dad if he's not speaking them? Maybe you'll need to take the first steps. Try this:

Begin talking to your dad. You've got to communicate. Doing the cold-shoulder thing causes roots of bitterness to flare up. And if you don't do anything about it, it may eventually be too late for that season, and you'll have all kinds of problems.

Shock your father's heart once in a while by saying, "I love you." I know it's hard for a teen guy, but instead of being on the defensive, try taking a proactive role and be the first to express what you want to hear back.

Choose your battles wisely. Understand that sometimes you're just not going to get your way. You have to compromise on some issues—and you have to honor the wishes of your parents. After all, God put you in their care.

Be willing to say you're sorry. When you blow it with Dad, be a man and admit it. Ask for forgiveness. That's one of the most important things in a healthy father/son relationship.

Pray. God fathers the fatherless. If your earthly dad does not fill the role, hope is not lost. Your dad may not be the kind of leader he needs to be. Understand that you're encountering a spiritual battle. Something unhealthy may be going on, but believe it: Love conquers all. And as you continue to work at finding God's love for him, finding ways to say or show "I love you," eventually he will realize, I love my son. While he's still alive, it's never too late. And even once he's gone, you can still learn to love him, understand him better, and forgive him.

• **PRAY IT OUT: "Lord, help me to have Your blessing."** Ask your heavenly Father to give you comfort and strength and grow you into His kind of masculinity. Ask Him to take your hand and protect you whenever the road ahead becomes dangerous.

TRIBAL MARKS

A KEY POINT I LEARNED TODAY:

HOW I WANT TO GROW:

MY PRAYER LIST:

A WARRIOR'S BATTLES

SEVEN STRATEGIES FOR CONQUERING LUST AND PORN

WEEK 3 ▶▶▶

SURVIVOR SECRETS

TRIBAL QUEST

Give up your secret struggles through confession and repentance.
EXPLORE THE WORD: Romans 7:14 - 8:17

TRIBAL TRUTH

So I find this law at work: When I want to do good, evil is right there with me. For in my inner being I delight in God's law; but I see another law at work in the members of my body, waging war against the law of my mind and making me a prisoner of the law of sin at work within my members. What a wretched man I am! Who will rescue me from this body of death? Thanks be to God—through Jesus Christ our Lord! So then, I myself in my mind am a slave to God's law, but in the sinful nature a slave to the law of sin. —**Romans 7:21-25**

TRIBAL FACE

Your Inner Gollum: Destroying "Precious"

"Malice eats it like a canker, and the evil is growing," Faramir, captain of Gondor, warns Frodo and Sam in J.R.R. Tolkien's *The Lord of the Rings*.

The stout warrior points to a repulsive creature traveling with the two hobbits. "He is wicked," the captain adds. "He will lead you to no good."

Gollum shrieks at Faramir's words, but Sam knows the captain speaks truth. *Why can't Frodo see this?*

Once known as Smeagol, Gollum possessed the One Ring—or, rather, he was possessed by it. And even today he burns with the desire to reclaim his "Precious."

"If we has it," Gollum tells himself, "then we can escape, even from Him, eh? Perhaps we grows very strong, stronger than Wraiths. Lord Smeagol? Gollum the Great? The Gollum! Eat fish every day, three times a day, fresh from the sea."

Sam doesn't trust Gollum. His thoughts wander back to a strange night in

DAY 15: STRATEGY 1—REVEAL YOUR SECRET STRUGGLES

the Dead Marshes. Sam awoke to discover *two Gollums*. Slinker and Stinker, as he had called them, were standing over Frodo, arguing with himself:

"Smeagol promised to help the master . . . ," Sam heard "Slinker" whine. *"Must have it,"* hissed "Stinker" in reply, his long-fingered hand slowly extending itself toward Frodo's neck. *"We wants it, we wants it, we wants it!"*[1]

On that eerie night, Sam had stopped Gollum just in time. But when Frodo woke up, his hobbit friend didn't cast Gollum away. Instead, Frodo looked upon the desperate creature with pity.

"I have to believe that he can come back," Frodo told Sam.

Long before Gollum was lured to the Forbidden Pool "by a mastering desire"—and well before the Ring had completely dominated the poor soul—Gollum was Smeagol, a gentle, hobbit-like being.

Today, as Frodo continues on his quest to destroy the Ring—with Sam by his side and Gollum leading them through the wilderness—Frodo shudders at a sobering reality: He, too, bears the same burden that had twisted Smeagol into Gollum.

Could this be my destiny? Is this what I will turn into if the Ring takes control?

It's hard to admit, but we can all relate to Gollum's struggle. Temptation hits and "Slinker and Stinker" begin waging a tug-of-war in our hearts. One voice screams, "Don't think—*just do it!*" Another whispers convicting words of truth and reason.

For most teen guys who struggle with lust and pornography, the internal battle often goes something like this:

Just one more time—and then I'll stop. It's not like I'm addicted.

Or am I?

This has gone on for a long time. Maybe I can't stop.

I know this is wrong, so why am I doing this?

What if I get caught?

Come to think of it, why am I acting so uptight? I'm a guy—and all guys do this. It's a testosterone thing. I'm not hurting anyone else. And if no one finds out, there's nothing wrong with it.

I'm not as bad as other guys. My life is so hard, it's different for me. This helps me cope.

But what does the Bible say? Will God forgive me? What if my parents find out? What if they already know? Maybe I should stop right now.

Stop being so paranoid. One more time won't hurt.

What if I am hooked?

Consider this warning from Luke 12:2-3: "There is nothing concealed that will not be disclosed, or hidden that will not be made known. What you have said in the dark will be heard in the daylight, and what you have whispered in the ear in the inner rooms will be proclaimed from the roofs."

Reveal your secret struggles—that's the first critical step toward conquering lust and pursuing purity. Being transparent with God, confessing your sins, and pursuing honest repentance will break the power of the "Precious" in your life. But if you hold on to a secret "mastering desire"—just as Smeagol hid in darkness, clutching the Ring—your heart and soul will eventually become as twisted as Gollum's. In other words, the evil you possess will end up possessing you.

TRIBAL TRAINING

• **Break the self-deception cycle.** Lust is nearly always accompanied by deceit. In other words, we can do bad things, yet we convince ourselves we are doing nothing wrong. According to author Patrick A. Means, an expert on addiction recovery, "When we want something badly enough, we'll deceive whomever we have to in order to get it. And the first person we have to deceive is ourselves." Means says we accomplish the self-deceit by telling ourselves two lies:

1. I don't really have a problem.
2. I can handle this alone.[2]

• **Strive to live without secrets.** There are two types of people in the world: those whose problems are visible to everyone around them and those who attempt to carry around secrets. Sadly, way too many Christian guys try to live in the second category, which ultimately puts them in the first category—usually at a cost: broken trust, ruined credibility, labels like *hypocrite*. Don't let a secret come back to bite you. Make a change now.

• **Confess your sins.** This is the healing answer to crippled faith and the way to bring your struggles into God's light. You don't have to live with a huge load of guilt and shame in your life. Christ is reaching out to you with open arms—go to Him in prayer. Tell Him all about your secret sins. Tell Him you're sorry, and He'll forgive you. "If we confess our sins, he is faithful and just and will forgive us our sins and purify us from all unrighteousness" (1 John 1:9).

• **Repent.** Once you've confessed the sin and asked Jesus to help you change (this is called *repentance*), stop flogging yourself. You're totally forgiven. Now, with your relationship fully restored with God, you can take steps toward growth and change. (The Holy Spirit will help you.)

• **Be warned: Avoid false repentance.** Sometimes guys shed tears of sorrow, promising God they'll never again commit a certain sin. Then, a few days, weeks, or months later—when temptation builds to a fever pitch—they find themselves falling back into the same sin again. "When it comes to giving up a secret life," Means says, "I believe there is a simple test to help us know whether we're experiencing true or false repentance. If I'm willing to tell someone else what I'm struggling with and ask for help, then it's true repentance. If I'm not willing to tell anyone else, I'm only fooling myself."[3]

• **Flee from temptation.** Everything you say, everything you do, every place you go, every thought you think is known by the Lord. Nothing can be hidden from Him. So, when you find yourself drawn to an immoral act—anything that would cause you to keep it secret from others—don't risk getting burned. Instead, take some advice from a firefighter:

STOP: Consider the consequences.

DROP: Get on your knees and pray.

ROLL: Run away from temptation.

• **Trust that when the pressure heats up, Jesus will intervene:** "No temptation has seized you except what is common to man. And God is faithful; he will not let you be tempted beyond what you can bear. But when you are tempted, he will also provide a way out so that you can stand up under it" (1 Corinthians 10:13).

• **PRAY IT OUT: "Lord, help me to live without secrets."** Ask God for the courage and strength to bring your struggles into the light.

TRIBAL MARKS

A KEY POINT I LEARNED TODAY:

_____

_____

_____

_____

_____

_____

HOW I WANT TO GROW:

_____

_____

_____

_____

_____

_____

MY PRAYER LIST:

_____

_____

_____

_____

_____

_____

SURVIVOR SECRETS

▶▶▶ **WEEKLY MEMORY VERSE**: *"For I know the plans I have for you,"* declares the LORD, *"plans to prosper you and not to harm you, plans to give you hope and a future."* —Jeremiah 29:11

TRIBAL QUEST

Trust that Christ loves you and will never give up on you—despite your sin and failures. Take the steps toward "de-shaming" your identity.

EXPLORE THE WORD: 2 Corinthians 5:14-21

TRIBAL TRUTH

Therefore, if anyone is in Christ, he is a new creation; the old has gone, the new has come! All this is from God, who reconciled us to himself through Christ and gave us the ministry of reconciliation: that God was reconciling the world to himself in Christ, not counting men's sins against them. And he has committed to us the message of reconciliation. —2 Corinthians 5:17-19

TRIBAL FACE

Bryce, 16
Kansas City, Missouri
De-Shaming His Identity

Seventeen-year-old Bryce leans forward, rests his chin on his knee, and listens carefully. He momentarily forgets about how crazy in love he is with Kellie—who just happens to be sitting right next to him. Pastor Jeff's talk is hard to swallow. Yet it does make sense.

"A lamp is useless if it's not plugged into its power source," the youth minister explains.

Suddenly, Pastor Jeff yanks a cord from an outlet, and the room goes completely black. Seconds later, someone clicks on another light—leaving bright squiggly lines dancing in front of Bryce's eyes.

"Did you know your faith is like a lamp?" Jeff asks. "Yet the sad fact is, too many of you not only have your 'switches' turned off—you're not plugged in at all."

A few groans and giggles roll through the room—even from Kellie. But Bryce doesn't laugh. He stares at the gray, lifeless bulb and thinks about his own faith.

God seems so far away, he tells himself, *and I feel so numb. I've messed up so badly, I'm at a point of no return. I mean, how can God forgive me now? How can He ever want me? My innocence is gone—my purity destroyed.*

Bryce glances at Kellie and begins feeling sick to his stomach. *I've messed up her life, too—yet she acts like everything's okay,* Bryce tells himself. *The parties, the drugs, the sex. We can't continue this way, but what's the point of changing?*

Jeff leans against the podium and looks right at him. "Tonight, I'm challenging each of you to plug back into the 'Source.' It's not too late. It never is with God. You can have a new beginning.

"Most of you know what a habit is," Jeff adds. "In fact, most of you are pros at cultivating them."

A couple of junior-high guys nudge each other and grin. Bryce's stomach knots up again. *Here it comes . . .* he tells himself. *A big dose of embarrassment. Bet he's gonna put me on the spot and make me say something dumb. I hate talking in front of crowds!*

The youth pastor continues, "I'm inviting you to develop a positive, transforming one—a habit called *faith*. It begins with trust in Jesus."

Jeff raises his hands in the air, like a child reaching up to his father. "Cry out to God. He's there. He won't reject you. Prayer is the key to plugging into Christ."

The pastor then holds up a Bible. "The next step is to get this truth into your heart," he continues. "Reading this book every day is one of the most important habits you can start. I challenge you to do it now. I guarantee you won't be like that lifeless light bulb."

Bryce leans against the wall, lets out a sigh of relief, then shuts his eyes. *Lord, I'm tired of feeling dark and miserable inside. I'm sick of the sin and shame. Help me start this new habit. And please . . . somehow . . . turn my light back on. Amen.*

As Jesus lived among us, He purposely engaged with those who were sexually immoral. His purity gave light to their darkness. He destroyed the grip of shame as He revealed the Father's love.

Yet, if you're honest with yourself, it's hard to grasp that, 2,000 years later, He won't give up on you. It's even harder to believe that in Jesus you'll find acceptance, love, and freedom—despite your shortcomings.

But like the woman in Luke 7:36-50—a sinner who was rejected and despised by the world—you've got to reach out to Jesus and trust His healing power.

TRIBAL TRAINING

• **Understand the battle that's being waged in your brain.** *I'm hopeless— too far gone—I can't change. I am what I am, and I'll always be this way.* Ever catch yourself thinking these thoughts? If so, you've bought a lie whispered into the hearts of young men by the Evil One. You're also trapped in a toxic shame cycle: You desperately want to change, yet you feel so flawed as an individual, you've concluded that you're "too far gone." So you buy Satan's lie that you're beyond God's help—continuing the cycle and enduring the battle.

The truth is, there's a big difference between *toxic shame* and *guilt*. Guilt has to do with our behavior, what we do; shame has to do with our identity, who we are. Author Patrick A. Means explains it this way in his book *Men's Secret Wars*: "When we do something wrong, our God-given conscience rings an alarm. That pang we feel is guilt. Guilt is not destructive to our person because we can do something about it. We can acknowledge our wrongdoing, change our behavior, experience forgiveness, and we no longer have to feel guilty. . . . [Shame] pools and swirls outside the fringes of our lives like a poisonous nerve gas, waiting for us to open the door a crack and let it seep in to paralyze and destroy. Shame, in this sense, is a demotivator for ongoing growth. It usually results in self-condemnation, discouragement, and the urge to give up."[4]

Toxic shame eats away at our core: *There isn't an ounce of good left in me. I'm so twisted and so bad, I simply cannot change. I'm hopeless, worthless, and rejected. God will never accept me.*

According to Christian counselor Robert S. McGee, toxic shame causes us to expect the worst from ourselves because we believe that's who we are inside. "We're not surprised when we disappoint people because deep down inside we know we're no good."[5]

• **Take the first step toward destroying toxic shame: Give God a chance.** Go to Jesus Christ in prayer and unload your secrets, your sins, and your shame. Tell Him every detail—just as if He didn't know a thing. Even though we covered confession and repentance in the Day 15 entry, spend some time today reflecting on your struggle with shame. Consider following this timeless advice from author and pastor Peter Marshall: "In [your conversation with Christ], be absolutely honest and sincere. Hold nothing back. Our minds are sometimes shocked when we permit our hearts to spill over, but it is good for our souls when we do. If we would only have the courage to take a good look at our motives for doing certain things we might discover something about ourselves that would melt away our pride and soften our hearts so that God could do something with and for us."[6]

- **The second step is to believe that Jesus Christ loves you and accepts you, despite your sin.** Best-selling author Max Lucado has a simple strategy for trusting God. In his book *He Still Moves Stones*, Max writes: "Take Jesus at His word. Learn that when He says something, it happens. When He says we're forgiven, let's unload the guilt [and shame]. When He says we're valuable, let's believe Him. When He says we're provided for, let's stop worrying."[7]

- **As you strive to be healed and made whole, wait patiently for the Lord.** "God is never in a hurry," Pastor Marshall points out. "Then when He speaks to you—as He will—do what He tells you. It generally comes through your own conscience—a sort of growing conviction that such and such a course of action is the one He wants you to take. Or it may be given you in the advice of friends of sound judgment—those whom you love the most. God speaks sometimes through our circumstances and guides us, closing doors as well as opening them. He will let you know what you must do, and what you must be. He is waiting for you to touch Him (see Mark 5:31). The hand of faith is enough. Your trembling fingers can reach Him as He passes. Reach out your faith—touch Him. He will not ask, 'Who touched me?' He will know."[8]

- **Along with your shame, unload the temptation to live with secrets.** Never believe the lie that you can ever say something, do something, go somewhere, or think things that God—and possibly others—won't know about. People who believe in secrets are people who get into trouble. Flip back to Day 15 and reread what we've written about giving up secrets.

- **Know that a pure mind is not necessarily a mind free of temptation.** A pure mind chooses to act in the right way when temptation strikes. Or, put another way, temptation is inevitable; what counts is how you meet it.

• **PRAY IT OUT: "Lord, show me how to shake the shame."** Ask your heavenly Father for His healing embrace. Pray that these truths go deep into your heart:

    1. You are not too far gone.

    2. Jesus loves you and accepts you.

    3. You are valuable in God's eyes.

▶▶▶CONSIDER TAKING TO HEART THIS PRAYER FROM CHRISTIAN SCHOLAR MARGARET CUNDIFF:

> *Lord, you know me. I am so set in my ways at times. I am stubborn, self-centered, and so sure I know it all. I must make you angry at times. Yet you love me, you are sorry for me, you want to give me so much. Give me the grace to admit when I am wrong, to turn from my self and accept your love, your way, your will.*[9]

TRIBAL MARKS

A KEY POINT I LEARNED TODAY:

_____

_____

_____

_____

_____

HOW I WANT TO GROW:

_____

_____

_____

_____

_____

MY PRAYER LIST:

_____

_____

_____

_____

_____

DAY 17: STRATEGY 3—EMBRACE FORGIVENESS

▶ ▶ ▶ **WEEKLY MEMORY VERSE**: *"For I know the plans I have for you," declares the LORD, "plans to prosper you and not to harm you, plans to give you hope and a future."* **—Jeremiah 29:11**

TRIBAL QUEST

Grasp Christ's forgiveness—then press ahead with the hope of His grace and freedom.

EXPLORE THE WORD: **Titus 3:1-11**

TRIBAL TRUTH

We lived in malice and envy, being hated and hating one another. But when the kindness and love of God our Savior appeared, he saved us, not because of righteous things we had done, but because of his mercy. He saved us through the washing of rebirth and renewal by the Holy Spirit, whom he poured out on us generously through Jesus Christ our Savior, so that, having been justified by his grace, we might become heirs having the hope of eternal life. **—Titus 3:3-7**

TRIBAL FACE

Jose, 15
Chicago, Illinois
Facing Judgment Day

The judge takes a deep breath, folds her hands, and looks Jose in the eyes. Suddenly, the 15-year-old boy knows he's in serious trouble.

His eleven other arrests had been a piece of cake: After a short stay at Chicago's juvenile-detention center, he was always released with a slap on the hand. Today is different. The court is actually talking about sending him away to a state youth jail.

The prosecuting attorney tells the judge he is a menace to society, while his public defender argues that he is a really nice kid who had made some mistakes. The teen's probation officer, on the other hand, throws up his hands and says he has given up on Jose. And now the boy's future is on the line.

Jose's mother breaks into tears as the judge bangs her gavel and confirms his worst fear: The court orders that he be committed to the Department of Corrections.

A sharp pain stabs Jose's stomach, and he suddenly has trouble breathing. *It's not supposed to turn out this way*, he tells himself. *These people are messing with Krazy J—a guy who is too sly, too tough, too lucky, and too cool to actually get caught. Only amateurs are sent to the state jail.*

Vandalism. Theft. Gang violence. Sexual conquests. As the cold, steel doors of his jail cell slammed shut, Jose couldn't help wondering if he'd ever get another chance. *How'd it end up this way? Why was I so stupid? And what about my life? Did I blow it for good?*

Jose isn't just a character who was dreamed up for this book. He's a *real* guy who joined a *real* Chicago gang—and ended up getting into some serious trouble. Check out his own words:

> The parties, the admiring girls, the missions against the opposition, the tall rank and respect I got when I beat up a rival gang member—gangbanging seemed exciting.
>
> But there was another side to this life nobody told me about when I joined. I saw my partners shot. Some were seriously wounded, others died. It tore me up to go to the funeral of a guy I'd grown up with.
>
> Then there were my buddies who were sent away to prison for nearly their entire lives—20, 30, 40 or more years. They even wanted to give one of my boys the death sentence. We're not talking fun and games now, but real tragedies with crying mothers, hurting sisters and weeping girlfriends.
>
> And now I was a part of it.

On the surface, Jose's life reads like every other gang tragedy reported in the news. But look behind the headlines, get to know Jose—and guess what? You suddenly realize that your own life isn't too different from his.

Like Jose . . .

. . . *You* are guilty of breaking the law—God's law.

. . . *You* will have your day in court—and will stand before the Ultimate Judge.

. . . *You* are completely forgiven—if you ask for it.

Several years back, a well-meaning father decided to teach his 14-year-old son a visual lesson about the consequences of sin. He'd just learned about his boy's struggle with pornography and wanted to intervene.

The father held up a two-by-four. "Notice the three nails in it?" he asked.

His son nodded.

"I'm going to pull out the nails," the father continued. "There! Now what do you see?"

"Holes," the son responded. "It's a worn two-by-four with three big holes in it."

"Exactly!" the father said. "It's the same way with sin in our lives. We may end up making mistakes that can hurt ourselves and others. And while we may be forgiven by those we've wronged, the holes will always be there. People will never forget what we've done."

A stern expression washed over the father's face as he locked eyes with his son. "So, the next time you're tempted to sin, think about the holes."

Question: Is this really how God works?

Are our mistakes like nails in a board that our Creator never forgets? Absolutely not! When we seek Jesus Christ and repent of our sins, we are fully forgiven.

True, we will face consequences for our actions—and, true, we may have scars that will take a lifetime to heal. Yet through the power of the Holy Spirit, we are washed clean and set free . . . and are given a new beginning.

Here's what the dad described above should have told his son: "The next time you're tempted to sin, think about the holes: The price Jesus paid on the cross. He'll give you the power to resist. He'll set you free from the slavery of sin."

• **Accept God's forgiveness.** Through the years, as I've counseled countless teenage boys who are battling lust and pornography, I've heard the same agonizing cry: "I'm just too bad to be a follower of Christ." Too many guys mistakenly believe that God won't forgive their sins.

Understand this: As sinners, we are all "foreigners" and "children of wrath." Yet, according to Ephesians 2, the Lord forgave our rebellion against Him. And even while we were still rejecting God, Romans 5:8 says that Jesus died for us. Get this: Christ looked down at those who nailed Him to a cross and cried out, "Father, forgive them, for they do not know what they are doing" (Luke 23:34).

Bottom line: God wants to forgive our sins so we can spend eternity with Him. (Check out Exodus 34:6-7.)

• **Learn from your mistakes.** It's every Christian's responsibility to practice avoiding the traps that cause you to stumble. A key verse to learn is Proverbs 26:11: "As a dog returns to its vomit, so a fool repeats his folly."

• **Look to the future.** Keep in mind that God isn't finished with you; the paint's still wet, and your faith's still under construction. Growing up in the Lord is a lifetime process. Check out Philippians 3:12: "Not that I have already obtained all this, or have already been made perfect, but I press on to take hold of that for which Christ Jesus took hold of me."

• **Strive to "walk in white."** Pursuing purity involves a spiritual process called sanctification: Through God's power, a believer is separated from sin and is dedicated to the Lord's righteousness. This is accomplished by the Word of God (John 1:1) and the Holy Spirit (Romans 8:3-4), and results in holiness, or purification from the guilt and the grip of sin.

Here's how Christian scholar Oswald Chambers explains it: "No one enters into the experience of entire sanctification without going through a 'white funeral'—the burial of the old life. If there has never been this crisis of death, sanctification is nothing more than a vision. There must be a "white funeral," a death that has only one resurrection—a resurrection into the life of Jesus Christ. Nothing can upset such a life; it is one with God for one purpose, to be a witness to Him. . . . This is the will of God, even your sanctification. When you realize what the *will* of God is, you will enter into sanctification as naturally as can be. Are you willing to go through that 'white funeral' now? Do you agree with Him that this is your last day on earth? The moment of agreement depends upon you."[10]

• **PRAY IT OUT: "Lord, I ask for Your forgiveness."** Ask the Lord to fill you with the peace of knowing that your sins are forgiven.

CONSIDER TAKING TO HEART THIS PRAYER FROM CHARLES HADDON SPURGEON:

What a mass of hideous sickness Jesus must have seen. Yet, He was not disgusted but patiently healed them all. What a variety of evils He must have seen. What sickening ulcers and festering sores. Yet He was prepared for every type of evil and was victorious over its every form. . . . In every corner of the field, He triumphed over evil and received honor from the delivered captives. He came, He saw, He conquered everywhere. . . . Whatever my case may be, the beloved Physician can heal me. Whatever the state of others whom I remember in prayer, I have hope in Jesus that they will be healed. My child, my friend or my dearest one, I have hope for each and all when I remember the healing power of my Lord. In my own situation, however severe my struggle with sin and infirmities, I too may be of good cheer. He who on earth walked the hospitals still dispenses His grace and works wonders among His children. Let me earnestly go to Him at once. [11]

TRIBAL MARKS

A KEY POINT I LEARNED TODAY:

_____
_____
_____
_____
_____
_____

HOW I WANT TO GROW:

_____
_____
_____
_____
_____

MY PRAYER LIST:

_____
_____
_____
_____
_____
_____

SURVIVOR SECRETS

TRIBAL QUEST

Understanding the scriptural metaphor of the Christian's armor is key in defeating the Goliath of sexual temptation.

EXPLORE THE WORD: **Ephesians 6:10-18**

TRIBAL TRUTH

Put on the full armor of God so that you can take your stand against the devil's schemes. —**Ephesians 6:11**

TRIBAL FACE

Your Inner Warrior
Suiting Up for Battle

The "armor of God" is something most believers have heard a lot about. We know we should put it on, and we know we should wear it all the time.

The big question is, how?

When it comes to putting on the armor of God, some people have a distinctly Harry Potter approach. First, they wave their Bibles around like some magic wand. Then they chant a few Bible words, to help the wand along: *Abracadabra, I now put on the belt of truth. . . . Shazam-bobwa, I now put on the breastplate of righteousness. . . .* The incantations continue down through the list.

And what's the sorry expectation from all this hocus-pocus?

Poof! Temptation goes away, forever—or at least for one day. And if these people keep putting their armor on, day after day, the devil will never get to them. *Make sure you get armored up. Satan knows if you've prayed those words today or not.*

That's just not real.

True Christianity is not an empty shell of formal religion: saying the right things, in the right way, at the right time. It's not about finding the "magic prayer" that will vanquish the Dark Lord of Masturbation once and for all. Whatever else true Christianity is about, it's about now. It's not about "the armor I put on during my quiet time this morning." That was sooo five hours ago! That Guess Jeans billboard you're driving by is right *now*!

True Christianity is about living truth in the moment. It's about enjoying Jesus in every second of the day. It's about warding off anything that threatens to take that enjoyment away, facing each attack as it comes.

If you don't appreciate the moment-by-moment nature of your relationship with Jesus, you'll spend a lot of time blaming God for not answering your prayer to take away your sexual desires, *once and for all!*

Ouch.

Are you really praying for that? They call it castration. With your guy mind being what it is, it probably wouldn't even work. You'd lose all the fun of sex and be left with the obsession.

Thankfully, it's also a prayer God won't answer.

What you really want is to learn to fight the battles as each one arises. That's true masculinity, by the way.

Paul's metaphor of the Christian's armor is an attempt to wrap truth in something easily remembered when those temptations attack. It's the truth behind the metaphor that brings you the victory, not the metaphor *itself*. Work the truth of the metaphor into your life through deep, consistent Bible study and meditative thought, and you're putting on the armor of God.

It's not an instant process, but true Christian growth never is.

TRIBAL TRAINING

Sexual temptation is a battle you can win. Sure, you've lost a few skirmishes — every man alive has. But your Captain's name is Jesus. Get a glimpse of Him. Let the "I-can't-lose-with-Jesus" mentality fill your soul (Philippians 4:13). You're a warrior. You're His warrior. And don't forget: Your Captain is also your armor.

In today's lesson, let's unwrap the metaphor, examining the truth behind it:

• **The Belt of Truth:** A Roman centurion's belt held his armor together. Without it, he was naked. Without it, he would never think of facing the enemy. And that belt had to be tight, "girded up," ready for battle. You need truth. The better your grasp of Scripture is, the bigger your belt buckle will be. Without it, you're naked, easy pickings for the enemy. And you need to continually cling tightly to Jesus, the living Truth (John 14:6), to be ready for battle. You can't fight sexual temptation alone.

• **The Breastplate of Righteousness:** The breastplate covered the chest. Without it, a soldier was open to a thrust in the heart. Satan goes for the heart, too. He tries to convince you that at the core, you're just a *wicked, sinful sex-fiend*, and that you have no choice to be anything but. That's just not true. In Jesus Christ, God sees you as *righteous* (2 Corinthians 5:21). When you believe what God says over what Satan says—*I am righteous because of Jesus; I am not wicked*—at that moment in time your breastplate is firmly in place, and you're protected from Satan's heart stabs at your identity.

• **The Gospel of Peace, Your Combat Boots:** A centurion's boots were carefully broken in and cared for. They were as much of a comfort during long days of travel as they were protection in battle. A lot of guys don't enjoy the Christian walk because they think it's a hard, long, impossible journey, especially concerning the subject of sexual temptation. But the message of Jesus is the good news of *peace*, not pain: "Come to me, all you who are weary and burdened, and I will give you rest. Take my yoke upon you and learn from me, for I am gentle and humble in heart, and you will find rest for your souls. For my yoke is easy and my burden is light" (Matthew 11:28-30). In those moments of navel-gazing discouragement, you don't have your combat boots on. Connect with Jesus. He's everything you need. The journey is not short, and sometimes it's even uphill— but it's an adventure that's meant to be enjoyed.

• **The Shield of Faith:** Jesus is also your shield (Psalm 84:11) and your faith (Galatians 2:20). Are you starting to get the picture here? A Christian's armor is nothing more and nothing less than a multi-faceted presentation of who Jesus is to you. If you need protection from sexual sin, you need more of Jesus. That's the upside of sexual temptation. It pushes you into a place where you're desperate to experience more of Him. And when those burning darts start flying—*Wow, look at that miniskirt over there*—you can raise your shield with a simple prayer: "Jesus, I need You!" Keep holding up the shield until those smoldering arrows get extinguished.

• **The Helmet of Salvation:** Do you think Jesus came merely to save you from the lake of fire? That's way *too narrow*. He also came to save you from *yourself*. His death handled the going-to-hell part, but His life is an ongoing miracle of salvation from the sinful cravings you were born with as a child of Adam (Romans

5:10). Salvation is life, abundant life, Jesus' gift to you (John 10:10). Every minute you're enjoying that abundance—that is, super-glad to be hanging out with Jesus—your helmet is on. And with that helmet firmly in place, your mind won't fall victim to the onslaught of sexy images in the cashier's aisle at Wal-Mart.

• **The Sword of the Spirit:** God's Word is your sword (Hebrews 4:12). It contains truth, and truth can stab at the heart of the lies of Satan. In a practical sense, it's easy to confuse this part of the armor with the belt of truth. One helpful distinction: The belt is for defense. But the sword of the Spirit is an offensive weapon. In your battle for sexual purity, there will be times when temptation will be so in your face, your best defense will be a strong offense. Quoting Scripture is the sword. Not a mindless, wave-the-magic-sword thing, but a heartfelt, specific application of Scripture—a well-guided thrust of God's Word. Job's words, "I made a covenant with my eyes not to look lustfully at a girl" (Job 31:1), have proven to be useful for many godly men over the centuries. There are many other passages that apply to sexual temptation. The more scriptures you memorize, the more skillfully you'll dispense with heavy attacks.

• **PRAY IT OUT: "Lord, help me to put on Your armor."** Ask Jesus to give you the strength and wisdom to fight your battle against lust.

TRIBAL MARKS

A KEY POINT I LEARNED TODAY:

_____

_____

_____

_____

_____

_____

HOW I WANT TO GROW:

_____

_____

_____

_____

_____

_____

MY PRAYER LIST:

_____

_____

_____

_____

_____

_____

_____

SURVIVOR SECRETS

▶ ▶ ▶ **WEEKLY MEMORY VERSE**: *"For I know the plans I have for you," declares the LORD, "plans to prosper you and not to harm you, plans to give you hope and a future." —***Jeremiah 29:11**

TRIBAL QUEST

In the battle for purity, you need an experienced soldier to fight alongside you. Find yourself a mentor.

EXPLORE THE WORD: **2 Timothy 1:1-2:7**

TRIBAL TRUTH

As iron sharpens iron, so one man sharpens another. **—Proverbs 27:17**

TRIBAL FACE

A Case of Spiritual Warfare
The Soul Slayer's Wicked Schemes

Two demons paced back and forth, unsure of what to do. The larger one rubbed his chin, staring at the ground as if trying to burn a trench under his feet. The other waddled along like a duckling, glaring at the glow from the nearby house. They stopped as their assigned target opened the window to the evening's breeze, his silhouette dark against the light of his room.

"He's impossible," growled the puny one. "I'm ready to ask for another mission, something less resistant than this saintly snake."

"Fool!" his partner snapped. "Has someone stuck you with a pitchfork? Our master would eat us for a midnight snack. We've got to find a way. "

"He's worse than a deaf bat," the little demon insisted. "He won't pay any attention to us. I bet he's studying his Bible right now." He stuck his head through the wall, confirming his suspicion. Then he jumped back, shivering. The enemy's Book did that to him sometimes.

"We still haven't tried that lovely temptation in his French class," he suggested. "She might bring him down."

The two exchanged glances, thrilled by the possibility. Then they shook their heads. Both knew that their target would only tell her about the enemy. Couldn't have that.

The two demons resumed their pacing. Suddenly, the dwarf demon spun on his head, giggling like a jackal. "I've got it!" the imp yelped. He stopped spinning and floated to his feet, savoring the moment.

His partner stared at him as if he'd joined the enemy. "What are you waiting for? Armageddon? Speak up!"

"Let's tempt him to live the Christian life by himself. We'll separate him from his pastor, his church friends, that Christian teacher of his. We'll convince him he doesn't need them. Let's make him an island, a super-Christian, a loner for God."

"You really do have a brain in that chicken-head of yours," the big fiend chuckled. "In three months, maybe six, our target will be so lonely and proud, he'll fall flat on his face. Then we'll have some fun with him."

The two demons huddled together to plan their attack.

So, you're gung-ho about your relationship with Christ.

You're reading the Bible, learning to pray, telling others about Jesus. You want to serve Christ with all your heart.

Great. Keep going. You're on the right track. Make it your life's journey to know and serve Him.

But don't do it alone.

Christians who go it alone make a big mistake. Without the support of other believers, we are prime targets for one of Satan's favorite tactics: isolate and conquer. We all need the input of other believers in our lives, especially that of older, more mature Christians.

One guy in the New Testament had the smarts to latch on to an older Christian named Paul. Timothy was perhaps 25 years younger than Paul, but he didn't let it scare him. In their long journeys together, they saw heathen temples and dark prisons, and they brought many people to Christ. Timothy picked up all kinds of great guidance from his coach, ranging from: "Don't let anyone look down on you because you are young" (1 Timothy 4:12), to: "Endure hardship . . . like a good soldier of Christ Jesus" (2 Timothy 2:3). Paul and Timothy were the closest trainer-trainee team in the entire Bible. Worth imitating, for sure.

So, be a Timothy. Give yourself some protection from Satan and a boost in your desire to live for Jesus. Find a Paul. Get yourself a mentor.

What's a mentor?

A mentor is a mature Christian guy with whom you can willingly share your dreams. A mentor is an encourager, someone whose advice you'd be happy to hear. A mentor is someone committed to seeing you reach your God-given potential in life.

A mentor is someone you would be wise to have.

TRIBAL TRAINING

- **Know what to look for in a mentor:**

  —Your mentor needs to be **available**. He should be someone who is willing to give you time. If he's always too busy to get together, look for someone else.

  —A mentor should be **a great listener**. Anyone who talks too much won't be much help.

  —You want a mentor who'll be **honest with you**. Sometimes your course in life will be off track. You need someone who'll be courageous enough to say so.

  —A good mentor is **transparent about his own struggles**. No mentor is perfect. Those who can admit their imperfections are worth more than those who hide behind an I've-got-it-all-together smile.

  —Most of all, a mentor should be **someone you admire**. But make sure you admire him for the right reasons: Just because he's an awesome skier doesn't mean he has the qualities you need. Look for godly character.

- **Know how to approach a prospective mentor:**

It's possible your mentor will come to you. Paul and Timothy were like that. Paul took the first step (see Acts 16:1-3). If that happens to you, take the relationship and run with it. It's more likely that you'll make the first approach, however. What you don't want to do is tap Joe Possibility on the shoulder and say, "Hi, will you be my mentor for life?" You may scare him off.

Instead, think about a problem or decision you're facing, something with which you need some help. Now pick a time and place you'd like to talk about it.

With these in mind, give your prospective mentor a call and say something like this: "I've got a problem I need some advice on. Could we get together? I'd really appreciate your help on this thing." If he says, "Sure!"—a high probability—suggest a time and place, and you're set.

Assuming the first meeting goes greater than you ever expected, try this before you part ways: "You've been really helpful. Could we do this again?"

There, you've found yourself a mentor. You're now an official "mentoree."

- **Know how to be a good mentoree:**

  —**Be punctual.** Most mentors are busy people. Don't waste his time by being late or failing to show up.

  —**Be outgoing.** Don't wait for your mentor to initiate the conversation. Come up with discussion topics before you get together. Let your mentor know what it is you expect in your relationship with him.

  —**Be open.** Share the bottom line in your life—your greatest pain, your deepest struggle. It's unlikely you'll shock your mentor with anything you've done. He's probably done it himself. You can't get help for things you hide.

  —**Be considerate.** Make sure the relationship with your mentor doesn't eclipse your growing friendship with Christ. If you let that happen, you'll become a leech that monopolizes your mentor's time. He should willingly give you his time, but he has his own life to live, too. Discover the healthy balance.

  —**Be hungry.** Ask questions, lots of them. Write down the answers. Tell your mentor if his advice helps. If it doesn't, let him know and invite more input. Watch your mentor—see what makes him tick. Find out how he and Jesus relate to each other.

  —**Be relaxed.** You're not going to solve all your problems in one sitting. Make sure you do both serious and fun things together. It's amazing how much you can learn on a fishing trip.

- **Know why having a mentor is vital to winning the battle with lust:**

  —**Guys need guy mentors.** Choose a woman, as godly as she may be, and you're asking for trouble. She'll make some young lady a great mentor, but not you.

—Realize God may have several mentors for you during the course of your life. Don't feel locked into having only one. People move; relationships change. Avail yourself of as many mentors as you reasonably can. Each will help you in different ways, at different times.

—Understand the ultimate goal of mentoring. Just before Paul died, he wrote Timothy these words: "And the things you have heard me say . . . entrust to reliable men who will also be qualified to teach others" (2 Timothy 2:2). The Christian life is meant to be a transformation from being a Timothy to being a Paul. Learn well the role of Timothy. With time, you'll become a Paul.

—One word of caution: There's a chance your relationship with a mentor might become destructive rather than helpful. If a mentor begins to control your life, or suggests something you know is a violation of God's Word, get out of the relationship—fast. It's a slim possibility. Be forewarned, but don't let the potential of one bad apple spoil the full barrel of good mentors who are out there.

Bottom line: *Don't be a loner for God.* Instead, look for the mentors God has lined up for you. No sense slashing your way through life's problems by yourself. There are many around who'll gladly help cut the trail. Be a Timothy. Find your Paul.

• **PRAY IT OUT: "Lord, bring a mentor into my life."** Ask God to connect you with a solid believer who will help sharpen your faith.

TRIBAL MARKS

A KEY POINT I LEARNED TODAY:

_____

_____

_____

_____

_____

_____

HOW I WANT TO GROW:

_____

_____

_____

_____

_____

_____

MY PRAYER LIST:

_____

_____

_____

_____

_____

_____

_____

SURVIVOR SECRETS

▶▶▶ **WEEKLY MEMORY VERSE**: *"For I know the plans I have for you," declares the Lord, "plans to prosper you and not to harm you, plans to give you hope and a future."* —**Jeremiah 29:11**

TRIBAL QUEST

Combine Bible reading with prayer, allowing Scripture to cleanse your heart.

EXPLORE THE WORD: **Hebrews 4:12 and 2 Timothy 3:10-17**

TRIBAL TRUTH

For the word of God is living and active. Sharper than any double-edged sword, it penetrates even to dividing soul and spirit, joints and marrow; it judges the thoughts and attitudes of the heart. —**Hebrews 4:12**

TRIBAL FACE

Eric, 15
Fort Walton Beach, Florida
Transformed by the Truth

"Hey, Bible Boy. Where's your Word?" shouts a voice from across the crowded hall.

Fifteen-year-old Eric grins and holds up a leather-bound book with big, bold words—*HOLY BIBLE*—printed on the cover. "Right here!" he calls.

It's Monday morning at Florida's Fort Walton Beach High School, and Eric loves his reputation. While other guys return from the weekend bragging about how far they've gone with a girl or how much they've drunk, Eric can't stop boasting about God . . . and how far Christ can take a life that's committed to Him.

It all started several months back when the teen made a decision about his life as a Christian: *It's all or nothing. No more goin' through the motions. No more phony faith. I'm sick of the same old struggles I've battled day after day. I want God to shape me into the man He created me to be.*

Eric's pastor began preaching about revival. A few of the wise Sunday-morning words stuck deep inside: "Christians who stay in their comfort zones will never experience radical transformation. They'll never see revival." The pastor pointed out that being committed to daily prayer and Bible reading is essential, referring to Romans 12:2: "Do not conform any longer to the pattern of this world, but be transformed by the renewing of your mind. Then you will be able to test and approve what God's will is—his good, pleasing and perfect will."

Eric knew he had to fix his own walk—which he sometimes thought of as a limp crawl. *I refuse to be defeated by lust and the crud of this world,* he told himself. *Jesus will win my battle with the flesh. I'm letting Him take control.*

"During one of our revival services, the Lord came and His Spirit poured out on our church. It was amazing," Eric says. "And when the pastor invited people to the altar, my friends and I all knew we needed to go forward."

The message from Revelation 3:15—about being lukewarm and wishy-washy—had touched a nerve. Eric realized that he wasn't on track with Jesus. He knew that real men of God take seriously Christ's commandment in Mark 12:30: "Love the Lord your God with all your heart and with all your soul and with all your mind and with all your strength."

"You have to *know* Jesus personally," Eric says. "He has to be your Best Friend—your Lord. You have to trust and obey Him. You have to study His Word, and let it saturate your heart."

"I thought about how half of my school wasn't even saved," Eric continues. "I knew I needed to make a change in my life, then reach out to other teens. I finally stood up and went down to the altar. Everything just broke. It was a real turnaround."

One of the first things Eric did was make a commitment to having a daily quiet time with God each day. The second—"and most important," he says—was to step out as a "walking billboard."

"Some teens wear Christian T-shirts and go to church, but they also spend their weekends partying and living a double life," Eric says. "I used to be that way, too."

Eric is convinced that if you're going to claim to be a Christian, you'd better be real with Jesus—both in public and in private. After all, being a walking billboard means having your life read by others. "I want people to read 'Jesus' when they see me," he says. "That's why I love being called Bible Boy. It's cool."

But being committed to Christ often comes at a cost. Eric lost a few friends who thought he'd become too religious, and he occasionally gets picked on.

What's more, Satan seemed to start working overtime, pushing many of his "sin buttons" and throwing old temptations back in his face. "Let's not kid ourselves; living for God is far from easy," Eric says. "But who says following Jesus *should* be easy?

"This world needs to see *real* Christians who have been transformed by God's Word," Eric says. "They need to encounter young men who are willing to stand in the face of temptation and popular culture and say, 'Jesus is the only Truth, the only Life, and the only Way.' "

Striving to live a life of purity and wearing the title "Christian" can feel like the world's most impossible task. (Hey, just ask Eric.)

Before we know it, we take our eyes off Jesus and begin to compromise in subtle ways—through our private thought life, our attitudes, our conversations, our relationships—and *wham!* We suddenly find ourselves acting anything but godly.

But as Eric discovered, what we really need is rock-solid security. Something that hangs in there even when everything else in our lives comes crashing down around us.

There's only one place to look—Jesus Christ.

When it comes to battling lust, many teen guys echo the same desperate plea: "It's like my problem is controlling me! I beg God to forgive me, and I even promise to stop doing what I don't want to do. But then I fail—again and again. *Help!*"

In each case, the real problem usually isn't what a teen guy thinks it is. (A struggle with lust is almost always just the symptom.) The *real problem* is actually *a heart problem*. And the only way to fix a mixed-up, sin-filled heart is through God's transforming touch. That means *spending time in the Word and in prayer*.

You see, the Bible is more than just a bunch of letters printed on paper. Scripture is living and active. Above all, it's God-breathed. There is a supernatural component to the Bible that saturates our hearts and shapes us into the men God wants us to be.

Combine Bible reading with prayer, and you've got a powerful weapon—an invisible sword, so to speak—that can fend off any deception and defeat any struggle that threatens to trap us.

I promise you this: In the days ahead, you'll be enticed by all kinds of temptations. But you can be a strong Christian who has the muscle to escape the lies and overcome the struggles. Follow this faith-building workout:

TRIBAL TRAINING

• **Commit to spending time every day reading Scripture and praying.** Stock up on an arsenal of devotional books that will guide you through the Bible.

• **Confess your struggles to Jesus as many times as you need to.** As I stressed in the Day 16 entry, Christ won't give up on you. Tell Jesus that you want to stop struggling silently and privately. Ask Him to go deep into your heart and heal the real wounds inside.

• **Seek a Bible-study partner.** Choose someone with whom you can share your deepest struggles; someone who will help you build strength through Christ.

• **PRAY IT OUT: "Lord, allow Your Holy Word to go deep into my heart."** Ask Jesus to cleanse and saturate your soul with the Truth.

TRIBAL MARKS

A KEY POINT I LEARNED TODAY:

_____

_____

_____

_____

_____

_____

HOW I WANT TO GROW:

_____

_____

_____

_____

_____

_____

MY PRAYER LIST:

_____

_____

_____

_____

_____

_____

SURVIVOR SECRETS

▶▶▶ **WEEKLY MEMORY VERSE**: *"For I know the plans I have for you," declares the L*ORD*, "plans to prosper you and not to harm you, plans to give you hope and a future." —*Jeremiah 29:11

TRIBAL QUEST

Temptation can attack at any moment, catching you asleep, spiritually. Learning to pray continually will keep you awake, on guard, ready to fight.

EXPLORE THE WORD: 1 Thessalonians 5:16-22, James 5:13-18

TRIBAL TRUTH

Be joyful always; pray continually; give thanks in all circumstances, for this is God's will for you in Christ Jesus. —1 Thessalonians 5:16-18

TRIBAL FACE

Manfred's Journey
How Prayer Shaped a Boy into a Man

As a teenager trying to serve Jesus, I (Manfred) used to take pride in how many Bible verses I'd memorized. I thought Bible memorization was the key to keeping God on my side.

With the perspective of years, I now realize that because of Jesus—not because of anything I've ever done—God's *always* on my side. Moreover, a head crammed full of the Bible doesn't necessarily equate with a heart full of Jesus. I learned that the day I heard about a guy who had memorized the entire book of Psalms and decided to keep being an *atheist*. Wow. That's what you call knowledge without understanding.

Anyway, back then I thought 1 Thessalonians 5:17 was a cool verse because it was so short, so easy to memorize: "Pray continually." Chalk up another verse for Manfred, the Super-Spiritual.

Talk about shallow Christianity.

In a more reflective moment, I heard God ask, *Okay, Manfred. What does that verse look like in real life?*

That stumped me. For me, prayer was that whole get-on-your-knees-and-hide-in-the-closet thing. I found myself muttering to God, "You want me to pray *all the time*? Like, when do I get to *eat*? Do I just *fast* to death? Don't you want me to do my *homework?*" Talk about limited, stuck-in-my-tiny-box thinking. That little verse got relegated to my commands-that-God-doesn't-really-expect-us-to-obey file.

I was 22 when I picked up a short book entitled *Practicing His Presence*. Wow! That book was core. It most convincingly described a life lived in the continual awareness of Jesus' presence. Brother Lawrence, the author, sought to spend every waking moment talking to, hearing from, and feeling the reality of Jesus in his life.

He had learned to *pray continually*.

What a mind-blowing, soul-overflowing concept!

From that book forward, my heart's deepest desire has been: *Enjoy Jesus all the time*. He's my happiness, my motivation, my peace, my reality —the Guy who listens to all my cranial conversation. I'm not real good at it—there are whole hours that go by when I completely forget about Him, but Jesus has a thousand cool ways of reminding me He's there. And occasionally—more frequently all the time—there are whole hours that go by where He and I can't stop talking.

When I first read that book, I was working in a factory full of pornography. Guys had it hung in their lockers, in the bathrooms, in front of their work stations. My machine had hardcore photos taped at eye level, six inches from my nose. The guy who worked my machine during the night shift hung them there, and I didn't think it was my place to remove them.

Gulp.

It was an amazing context in which to learn to pray continually. It was a stumbling process—I can remember at least half a dozen times where I gave up fighting temptation—but it was a growing process, too. After almost two years working in that factory, I experienced several days where God and I talked *the whole shift*.

Eight hours straight, nonstop.

To this day, I have a hard time praying even one hour on my knees, let alone all day. But that isn't what God requires.

He's asking me to *pray continually*. Thanking Him for a new day the first instant I wake up. Asking Him for strength when I stumble into the bathroom. Praising Him for good health during my morning push-ups. Trusting Him for a day of purity while I'm in the shower. Imagining myself "putting on Jesus" as I pull my pants on. Enjoying God's gift of food with each bite of breakfast. Telling God, *I'm hungry now*, as I open my Bible. Begging Him for guidance as I type these words. . . .

Are you grabbing this? Are you ready to run with this?

It's *possible* to pray continually. You've got to want it. It takes practice. But it's so very possible. And once you start to taste the wonders of a life in constant touch with Jesus, you'll want more.

And more.

Jesus promised you an abundant, exciting life. Praying without ceasing is how you tap in to that life.

And as one of many side benefits to *practicing His presence*, you'll find yourself winning more and more of those battles with Miss Way-Too-Tight-Pants, the girl whose locker is right across from yours.

During every moment of your waking existence, your mind is in continual conversation. That's what thoughts are: internal mind speak. You're talking to someone, right now, in your head.

The problem is, most of the time you're talking to yourself.

What a boring way to live.

With a small shift of the mind, a little trigger called "faith," you can direct that internal conversation to Jesus. Instead of talking with yourself via your thoughts, you can engage Jesus in them.

That's prayer. That's praying without ceasing. Praying is as simple as directing your thoughts to Jesus.

What does that really look like?

Imagine a scenario. It's 6 A.M. You were up late last night. It's time for your Saturday-morning shift as cashier at the local 24-hour Whataburger. You stare into your bathroom mirror. You're in rough shape.

Got the picture? Ever been there?

Now, let's look at this scenario first from the eyes of someone who has learned nothing about practicing the presence of Jesus:

Ouch, my aching head. This is awful. How am I going to survive this rotation of the earth? I feel like week-old roadkill. Is there anyone here who wants to call in sick today? That would be me. Man, where is my toothpaste? Is the light on?

Yes, I think so. But I can't even see!

This is going to be an ogre of a day.

Now, let's take that same person, same circumstances. One difference, though. This person has now learned to *pray continually*. Let's see what that might look like:

Ouch, Lord, my head is really sore. Anything You could do for me? Yeah, right. Hanging out until 3 A.M. isn't always the smartest thing to do, is it? Well, anyway, I've gotta survive this next rotation of the earth. I feel like week-old roadkill. How's that? You want me to 'more than survive'? You want me to keep my eyes on You? You're my strength? My joy? Right, I'm getting it now. You had some long nights and early mornings, too, didn't You? And You were never a miserable ogre. Sure would be tempting to call in sick, though. Naw, that wouldn't do much for my reputation. It would kind of reflect badly on You, too, wouldn't it, Jesus? All right, let's get this thing done together, Lord. Give me some of that strength and joy.

By the way, Lord, I can hardly see, even though I'm pretty sure the light's on. Can You help me find my toothpaste?

So, which of those two would you rather be? The choice is yours. Right now. This moment. Start praying.

And keep praying.

TRIBAL TRAINING

• **Know what prayer is.** It's not just going through the motions, saying a bunch of thoughtless, mechanical words—as some people do when they give thanks for a meal. It is actually communicating with the One and Only eternal God. "He is the incredible God who created everything there is, and who is in control of the universe, which is expanding at the rate of 186,000 miles a second in all directions every hour," writes Kenneth N. Taylor in his book *How to Grow*. (Kenneth is a popular scholar who is famous for *The Living Bible*.) "You, as God's child, can come right into His presence where He joyfully welcomes you because you have become His."[11]

• **Stop making excuses—just do it!** It's amazing when Christian guys (or adults) make lame excuses such as, "I don't know what to say," or "I don't know how to pray!" If you've figured out how to talk to a friend on the phone or how to send e-mail on the Internet, then you know how to pray. Jesus is your Best Friend, and He wants you to tell Him about everything that's going on in your life. He wants to know the desires of your heart, how badly you feel when you fail, how happy you are when good things happen. And while the Bible tells us to pray always and for any reason (see Ephesians 6:18), Jesus has also demonstrated the importance of getting alone to pray (see Matthew 26:36-39.)

• **Get alone with God.** Find a private place—anywhere: your bedroom, the kitchen table while everyone else is asleep, an undisturbed corner of your school's library—and carve out a block of "quiet time" every day for prayer. Exactly what time you do this and for how long is up to you. The key is to have some time alone with God so that you can give Him your undivided attention. A committed, unhurried quiet time is actually the most important part of a Christian's day.

It's your time to . . .
. . . let go of your fears and worries.
. . . listen to God's instruction.
. . . praise your awesome Creator.
. . . pray for friends and family.
. . . power up with the Holy Spirit.

• **PRAY IT OUT: "Lord, show me how to be a man committed to prayer."**
Ask God to help you pray continually.

TRIBAL MARKS

A KEY POINT I LEARNED TODAY:

_____
_____
_____
_____
_____
_____

HOW I WANT TO GROW:

_____
_____
_____
_____
_____
_____

MY PRAYER LIST:

_____
_____
_____
_____
_____
_____
_____

A WARRIOR'S BATTLES

MARKS OF A BATTLE-READY WARRIOR

SURVIVOR SECRETS

▶ ▶ ▶ **WEEKLY MEMORY VERSE**: *But you are a chosen people, a royal priesthood, a holy nation, a people belonging to God, that you may declare the praises of him who called you out of darkness into his wonderful light. Once you were not a people, but now you are the people of God; once you had not received mercy, but now you have received mercy.* —1 Peter 2:9-10

TRIBAL QUEST

Your desire to win the war against lust is part of a bigger picture: holiness. Don't get fixated on one single area of your life.

EXPLORE THE WORD: 1 Peter 1:13-16; 2 Peter 1:3-8

TRIBAL TRUTH

But just as he who called you is holy, so be holy in all you do; for it is written: "Be holy, because I am holy." —1 Peter 1:15-16

TRIBAL FACE

Peter
A Salty Sea Dog

Peter was once a rough fisherman. Like your average sailor of the day, the guy had cusswords on his lips and murder in his heart. After three years with Jesus, he'd learned a few things, but he was still full of brash bravado, the kind that posers-who-think-they're-tough carry. He thought he was ready to die with Jesus.

Boy, did Peter have a lot to learn.

One night, when Jesus was arrested, Peter finally saw what he was truly made of. Not real impressive.

Peter first tried to kill the high priest's servant, Malchus, in an effort to keep Jesus from being arrested. Peter saw himself as a one-man hostage rescue team. Good thing he was really just a wannabe swordsman. He only managed to cut the guy's ear off.

Good thing, too, that Jesus was a Master Healer.

After that, the big blowhard darts into the dark like a midnight shadow on a moonless night. Full of mixed, wimpy feelings, Peter later follows the mob that arrested Jesus, but he does so from a distance. Jesus is in trouble, and Peter doesn't want it rubbing off on him. When they reach the high priest's courtyard, some servant girl insists she's seen him with Jesus. Peter gets all mad and denies the fact using the Jewish equivalent of four-letter words.

Then Peter bawls his eyes out and decides that his Savior and Friend is a dead goner, even though Jesus told him several times He would rise from the grave. With the whole city buzzing around Jesus' arrest and crucifixion, Peter ducks the pressure; he goes to lay low in a house, hiding out like a toad under a rock.

This is Jesus' disciple *numero uno*. What a disaster.

Peter was a married man, with a mother-in-law and everything (Matthew 8:14). Though the Bible doesn't specifically mention Peter having sexual issues, it's safe to assume that this rough fisherman struggled like any normal guy. At the very least, he would have had to keep his eyes from straying while in town selling the day's catch. The Jewish market had prostitutes, just like anyplace else.

It's amazing this loser who reminds us so much of ourselves eventually wrote two books of the Bible. This smelly, hairy grunt, who liked to have it all hang loose while slinging his nets, wrote something as high-minded as this: "Make every effort to add to your faith goodness; and to goodness, knowledge; and to knowledge, self-control; and to self-control, perseverance; and to perseverance, godliness; and to godliness, brotherly kindness; and to brotherly kindness, love. For if you possess these qualities in increasing measure, they will keep you from being ineffective and unproductive in your knowledge of our Lord Jesus Christ" (2 Peter 1:5-8).

Whatever else Peter finally learned, he understood two huge things: The Christian life is a multi-faceted experience, and it's all about our Lord Jesus Christ.

As a young man desiring purity, you probably noticed one quality in Peter's list: self-control. You want self-control. You're tired of having your passions go way *out of control*. You want to see God bring them under *His* control.

That's a good, healthy desire you want to nourish and aim for.

But if it's the only goal in your walk of faith, you have an unhealthy fixation. Your goal in life is not merely to stop thinking filthy thoughts. That's like being told: *Stop thinking about pickle-flavored ice cream. Don't visualize those tiny pieces of pickle mixed into the cream. Don't imagine how gross that would taste. Nope, don't think about it.*

The more you're told you should stop, the more you think about it. If that's mildly true of ice cream, it's totally true about gorgeous women.

When it comes to overcoming the challenge of sexual temptation, you need a bigger goal than being told, "STOP LOOKING AT BEAUTIFUL BABES!" You need something that will keep your heart, mind, and body so busy with good things, you won't have headspace or hormones for the bad things.

So, what's the goal?

Holiness. No, wait a minute: The goal is Jesus. No, both.

The fact is, they're one and the same.

Jesus is holiness in three dimensions. "Holy, holy, holy" is how the angels describe Him. Jesus, God's holiness in human flesh, needs to be your fixation (Hebrews 12:2). And God's Son is a totally healthy fixation, one that can capture your whole being and fill it with mission, desire, joy, and fulfillment.

Holiness may sound boring, impersonal, unreachable. That's understandable.

Jesus, on the other hand, is totally exciting, totally personal, totally right there. And making Him your complete focus will touch every area of your life.

You don't merely want to stop drooling at the beach. You want to see women through the eyes of Jesus. You don't simply want to shatter that late-night TV habit. You want to go to sleep talking to Him, He who committed no sin. Your goal is bigger than stifling that heart attack whenever you see a *Maxim* mag across the store. You want the Prince of Peace *all* the time.

You really do.

TRIBAL TRAINING

• **Let God begin a work in you.** The Lord, in His desire to make you holy, is going to work with you as a *whole* being. He'll teach you about faith, goodness, knowledge, perseverance, godliness, brotherly kindness, and love—as well as self-control.

So, if you want to get masturbation under control, but also have a problem with laziness, be prepared. God's going to teach you about hard work, setting goals, and filling your life with healthy activity.

• **Let God take you out of your comfort zone.** If you're trying to fill your void with phone sex, and at the same time you have a problem with getting out and meeting others, God's got something for you. He'll take you out of the false comfort of your four walls and teach you to find your sense of safety in Him. At the same time, He'll show you that you can enjoy people without constant fear. And if they hurt you in some way, He'll teach you to forgive.

• **Let God give you a fresh mindset.** If you're sick of rubbernecking every girl who walks by, but would rather play *Halo 2* than read your Bible, get ready for a fresh look. God will do all He can to prove to you that His Word is relevant, interesting, and more soul-satisfying than this year's greatest Game Boy release.

• **Let God deal with you as a whole being: body, soul, and spirit.** The Lord will deal with you as such, because all three aspects of your being are interconnected. The discipline you exercise in getting up to run three miles every morning will overlap and assist with your desire to study God's Word each day. Your honesty as student-council treasurer will help you tell the truth when your mentor asks how the purity thing is going. The decision before God to stop overeating—and maybe even fast once in a while—will help you to not indulge in the sexual realm, as well.

• **Let God instill in you a new definition for *holiness*.** In its simplest definition, it means "wholly set apart for God." So, don't offer Him just your libido. Offer Him your whole being. You can't put those things in better hands.

• **PRAY IT OUT: "Lord, help me to be holy, as You are holy."** Ask Jesus to show you what holiness looks like and how you can live it out practically day by day.

TRIBAL MARKS

A KEY POINT I LEARNED TODAY:

_____

_____

_____

_____

_____

_____

HOW I WANT TO GROW:

_____

_____

_____

_____

_____

MY PRAYER LIST:

_____

_____

_____

_____

_____

_____

SURVIVOR SECRETS

▶▶▶**WEEKLY MEMORY VERSE**: *But you are a chosen people, a royal priesthood, a holy nation, a people belonging to God, that you may declare the praises of him who called you out of darkness into his wonderful light. Once you were not a people, but now you are the people of God; once you had not received mercy, but now you have received mercy.* —**1 Peter 2:9-10**

TRIBAL QUEST

Only truth can topple the strongholds Satan has constructed in your mind. Truth is a battering ram you need to grab hold of. When the lies about sex get knocked down, Satan won't have a base from which to attack you.

EXPLORE THE WORD: **2 Corinthians 10:3-5**

TRIBAL TRUTH

Do not conform any longer to the pattern of this world, but be transformed by the renewing of your mind. Then you will be able to test and approve what God's will is—his good, pleasing and perfect will. —**Romans 12:2**

TRIBAL FACE

Paul
Prisoner of Christ

Before Paul the apostle, there was Saul the Pharisee. Saul was a Satan-programmed terminator for the early Christian church.

Long before Saul decided to imprison and kill Christians, the Deceiver was at work, building a huge stronghold of lies in Saul's mind. The devil's building blocks came from many sources: the people's gossip about Jesus, the jaded opinions of his fellow Pharisees, a host of twisted Scripture interpretations, and even his own obey-the-letter-of-the-law zeal. It all helped build a dark fortress in Saul's mind. By the time he gave the order to have Stephen stoned to death, that stronghold was high and mighty, a huge base of operations for Satan's bigger plan of wiping Christianity off the face of the earth.

Thankfully, Jesus smashed that fortress to smithereens one day while Saul, the soon-to-be apostle Paul, was on the road to Damascus. All the lies Saul believed about Jesus came tumbling down with the question, "Saul, Saul, why do you persecute me?" (Acts 9:4). Jesus, the Truth, is an amazing battering ram.

Paul, the most intellectual of the New Testament writers, understood how Satan works in the mind. In 2 Corinthians 10, Paul wrote about strongholds that seek to keep you from obeying Christ, strongholds that need demolishing. If you understand the same things Paul did, Satan will have a tough time defeating you in your desire to follow Jesus.

The first thing you need to understand is that Satan's lies aren't random events. He carefully chooses and lays down each lie like a master mason building a castle. And Satan's lies aren't occasional events. It takes a lot of lies to build a fortress. He's trying to lay blocks in your mind a thousand times a day.

These days, Satan has a host of rock quarries from which he can get building material: TV, magazines, music, teachers, professors, libraries, the Internet, misguided preachers, equally misguided friends, your own crazy thoughts—you name it.

Once Satan finishes building a stronghold in your mind, he finds it easy to launch flaming arrows from behind those walls—close-range attacks designed to make you fall in specific situations. For example, having built the fortress of *"Sex before marriage is no big deal"* in your mind, Satan can now launch the burning dart, *"There's Charlotte: big, beautiful, and ready for bed. Go for it."*

Understand that the stronghold and the flaming arrows (Ephesians 6:16) are both made up of lies. Satan uses building-block lies to set himself up for the real attack—flaming-arrow lies intended to pierce and burn you to the ground.

Now, here's the scary part: Satan has *already* built a mess of fortresses in your mind. If you're 18 years old, he's had exactly that many years to build them. The size and number of strongholds in your mind depend on several factors: the circumstances of your upbringing, the quality of Bible teaching you've received, your level of exposure to worldly ideas, and most importantly, the amount of truth you've absorbed—or not.

Regardless of how those factors add up, Satan has free reign *somewhere* in your mind. Right now. Like a guerilla, the devil sneaks around behind the walls he's constructed, sniping at will.

Jesus wants to locate those strongholds for you. He wants to show you just how many lies you've come to believe. Then, having targeted a given stronghold, your Savior and Captain wants to shatter it with truth. And once that target is obliterated, Jesus will right away aim for the next stronghold.

But you've got to *want* it. Bad. No want, no happen. Big want, big happen.

Jesus is definitely the Captain, but for some reason, He's allowed you to be the General of your own mind. You give the orders. You want a stronghold targeted? You want to turn it to rubble? It's your call. Or would you rather leave it there because you don't want to fight the battle? That's the default choice, and it's completely yours to make.

So, are you going to fight the battle of wiping out the strongholds in your mind? It's your choice. Choose well.

No magic wands, though, remember? Generally, truth does not tumble in one instant the strongholds that Satan has taken years to build. Truth needs to be applied constantly and patiently, like a battering ram.

In real life, it might look like this:

> *Wow, Lord, that magazine rack is drawing me like a black hole, sucking me into its vortex. I don't feel like I can break free. But I can do everything through him who gives me strength, right? Philippians 4:13. Great verse. Thanks, Lord. Let's just check out this next store over here.*

> *Uh, oh. There's Charlotte. What is she doing here? Yeah, right, it's the mall—and she's a girl. But did she have to come now? That skirt is sooo short. And those legs are sooo fine. "I made a covenant with my eyes not to look lustfully at a girl!" Where'd that verse come from? Is that Job yelling down from heaven, Lord? Whatever. Sounds like a good plan. I'd love to take another peek, but, uh, let's not.*

> *What am I doing in the mall right now, anyway? Just because it's Saturday? I'm wasting time. Doesn't your Word say something about being very careful about how I live, making the most of every opportunity? Somewhere in Ephesians 5, right? Let's get out of here, Lord. This day is an opportunity to do some something useful. I don't want to lose it.*

> *Wait a minute, Jesus. Can you help me remember where I parked the car?*

• **Arm yourself with the truth.** God's Word needs to be faithfully and meaningfully applied to real life in order to see those strongholds smashed out of existence. Consistency is key. Every choice is one of bashing Satan's buildings or letting Satan build. Without consistency in your life, Satan can rebuild partially crumbled walls. You don't want that to happen.

• **Pray. Read. Meditate.** Paul put it this way in Romans 12:2: "Be transformed by the renewing of your mind." All that garbage thinking needs to be replaced with fresh truth. Sort out what's in your head. Target the strongholds. Batter those strongholds to pieces. Take the garbage out and trash it. Then fill your mind with the good, pleasing, and perfect *Word* of God, which will quickly take you to the good, pleasing, and perfect *will* of God. It's your choice. Get thirsty for truth. No want, no happen. Big want, big happen.

• **PRAY IT OUT: "Lord, let my entire being thirst for truth."** Ask God to transform your heart, mind, and soul.

TRIBAL MARKS

A KEY POINT I LEARNED TODAY:

_____

_____

_____

_____

_____

_____

HOW I WANT TO GROW:

_____

_____

_____

_____

_____

_____

MY PRAYER LIST:

_____

_____

_____

_____

_____

_____

SURVIVOR SECRETS

▶▶▶ **WEEKLY MEMORY VERSE**: *But you are a chosen people, a royal priesthood, a holy nation, a people belonging to God, that you may declare the praises of him who called you out of darkness into his wonderful light. Once you were not a people, but now you are the people of God; once you had not received mercy, but now you have received mercy.* —**1 Peter 2:9-10**

TRIBAL QUEST

Jesus Christ demonstrated the most awesome display of self-sacrificing humility the world has ever seen. Guys who are serious about walking the path to purity will stomp out pride and follow Christ's example.

EXPLORE THE WORD: **Philippians 2:1-11**

TRIBAL TRUTH

Do nothing out of selfish ambition or vain conceit, but in humility consider others better than yourselves. —**Philippians 2:3**

TRIBAL FACE

Scott, 16
Redding, California
Following Christ's Footsteps

Scott opens his eyes and squints. Light is streaming through the blinds of his bedroom window. It's morning— Monday morning, a school day. It's time to start another week of hectic routines: homework, exams, football, youth group.

But instead of burying his head in a pillow and groaning or pleading with his mom for another minute of sleep, this 16-year-old young man feels different today. He's strangely energized, freed from Satan's strongholds; ready to embrace a new day—a new direction for his life.

Scott throws off the covers and sits up. A verse he studied in Sunday-night Bible study races through his mind, reminding him of a sacred vow he had made: "For the eyes of the LORD range throughout the earth to strengthen those whose hearts are fully committed to him" (2 Chronicles 16:9).

Lord, I mean what I promised: It's all or nothing, he prays silently. *No more going through the motions. No more living for myself. I want to be Your servant, a man whose heart is fully committed to You. Give me the strength to start fresh. Give me the courage to follow in Your footsteps.*

Scott learned from his youth pastor that God is most interested in the condition of a young man's heart. "In Acts 13:22, the Lord described David as a man after His own heart, someone who will 'do everything I want him to do,' " Pastor Cleary had explained. "Can God count on you? Are you such a man?"

The questions pierced deep into Scott's own heart. Right there, in the middle of the Bible study, he fell to his knees in prayer—confessing his sins and vowing to be God's warrior. "Lord, my life is not right with You, but I want it to be," he said, tears rolling down his cheeks. "I'm sorry for my sins. I've not been pure of heart: I've struggled with porn and lust. My heart has been so clouded with pride that I've disobeyed my parents, and I've been a poor example to my brother and my friends. . . ."

When Scott finished praying, the other five guys in the group followed his lead, forming a football-style huddle and confessing their sins, too.

A short time later, Pastor Cleary began to read from Philippians 2:5-11: "Your attitude should be the same as that of Christ Jesus: Who, being in very nature God, did not consider equality with God something to be grasped, but made himself nothing, taking the very nature of a servant, being made in human likeness."

With arms still linked and heads bowed, the guys reflected on every word. The passage had become their creed—an example of Christ's radical love and humility that would transform their hearts.

"And being found in appearance as a man, he humbled himself and became obedient to death—even death on a cross! Therefore God exalted him to the highest place and gave him the name that is above every name, that at the name of Jesus every knee should bow, in heaven and on earth and under the earth, and every tongue confess that Jesus Christ is Lord, to the glory of God the Father."

"Amen," the pastor declared, closing his Bible.

"AMEN!" shouted the group.

Twelve hours later, Scott knows that the first steps he must make involve setting things straight with the most important people in his life:

HIS PARENTS

"Mom, Dad—I love you so much," he tells them at the breakfast table. "I'm sorry for never saying those words and for giving you a hard time. I'm sorry for being so prideful. I really want to be different."

Scott's mom reaches over and feels his forehead. "Honey, are you feeling okay today?"

The teen cracks a smile. "Better than ever!"

HIS BROTHER

Scott glances at his younger brother—who suddenly chokes on a big gulp of orange juice. "Stay back," blurts his brother. "I don't want to catch whatever it is you have!"

"Actually, you need to," Scott laughs. "God is doing something really cool in my heart, and I hope it's contagious. I want to be there for you. I hope the Lord touches your life through me."

HIS GIRLFRIEND

Before classes start, Scott pulls his girlfriend aside and takes her hand. "I'm so sorry," he says.

"For what?" she asks. "You haven't done anything wrong."

"I've taken for granted the amazing person God created you to be," he explains. "All this time, I've been so selfish. Even though I tell you that I love you, my heart has been so impure. Whenever I look at you, I only think of myself—how much you please me."

His girlfriend suddenly looks puzzled. "But Scott, we don't have anything to be ashamed of," she says. "I mean, we make out like every other couple, and we've gone a little too far in the past, but I know you care about me."

Scott leans closer and kisses her forehead. "I care deeply about you, which is why things have to be different now. Our love has to be real. We have to put God first, then each other. We have to make a commitment to purity."

His girlfriend nods her head and smiles.

HIS BEST FRIENDS

"Football, parties, and popularity don't matter to me anymore," Scott tells two of his football buddies. "Only one thing counts in life: Committing our hearts to Jesus and living for Him."

Then Scott does something his friends will never forget: he hugs them both, looks them in the eyes, and says, "I love you."

One of Scott's friends speaks up: "I have to ask you something," he says. "Is this a 'God thing'?"

"Yes," Scott says, "it's definitely a God thing."

Instead of thinking Scott has gone off the deep end mentally, his buddies actually begin to respect him.

HIS FOOTBALL COACH

Next, Scott quits the football team at the high school he attends.

"Frankly, I'm shocked by your decision," says Scott's coach, Mark Pettengill. The coach looks the boy in the eyes and asks, 'Scott, you're very talented— why?'

"Because I need to use the time I spend practicing, getting closer to God."

In the days ahead, Scott is never seen at school without his Bible. And he is always decked out in blue jeans and a white T-shirt. He tells everyone he meets, "White stands for purity."

"He really desires to be a godly guy and a solid example to others," says Pastor Cleary. "His brother began to follow in his footsteps. But trust me, they have never stopped being a couple of zany guys. Whenever you see the two, they have giant smiles stretched across their faces, or they pop off with jokes. And one of Scott's favorite activities is to T.P. someone's house (always someone he knows and loves)."

On campus, many students and faculty begin to take notice of Scott's radical new walk. According to Scott's English teacher (and a Christian who helped Scott start a lunch-hour Bible study), Scott is a committed clique-buster.

"He doesn't hang out with just the popular people," she says. "He befriends everybody—especially the underdogs. People really respect him for that."

Scott and his brother even spend time at a local soup kitchen, witnessing to the homeless.

"God put a flame in Scott," one student notes. "And Scott shared it with his brother. Through the two of them, it grew.

"And as they shared with others, it turned into a campfire—and just kept right on growing. Today, Scott's flame is a bonfire."

Scott was determined to give up phoniness. He set out to live Philippians 2:3: "Do nothing out of selfish ambition or vain conceit, but in humility consider others better than yourselves."

Above all, Scott desperately wanted to be the kind of Christ-built warrior his pastor had described: "Your character is who you are when no one is looking and what you are willing to stand for when someone is looking. A true man of God desires to obey his Creator with all his heart, mind, and soul."

Scott's first steps involved stomping out pride and following Christ's example of humilty. His decision, and the choices he made, profoundly influenced those around him.

Pride and selfishness struggle desperately to elbow humility and purity out of our lives. While no one has escaped their grip completely, not many guys have the guts to be like Scott—freely admitting that they are guilty of this sin. Some teens will 'fess up to other vices—a bad temper, a struggle with lust, an addiction—yet, somehow, a problem with pride is often overlooked.

C.S. Lewis, on the other hand, challenges us to take pride very seriously. "The essential vice, the utmost evil, is pride. Unchastity, anger, greed, drunkenness, and all that, are mere flea bites in comparison: it was through pride that the devil became the devil. Pride leads to every other vice: it is the complete anti-God state of mind."[1]

Lewis describes pride as "spiritual cancer" and warns that its presence in our lives can block us from knowing God. His observations ring true in the life of a Pennsylvania teen I recently met. This young man came to me for advice.

"No matter how hard I try, I just can't seem to stop swearing," he explained. "I've prayed and prayed and have even gone to my parents about it. They just quote Scripture, and tell me to make new friends and stop listening to certain kinds of music. I don't want to make new friends, and I love my style of music. I don't listen to it because of the profanity; I just like it. And to be honest, I love the Lord, but I'm not really interested in reading the Bible. What do you suggest I do?"

I leaned back and scratched my head. "Let me get this straight," I responded. "You say you've 'prayed and prayed' about your problem . . . and that you've even gotten some scriptural answers, yet you don't like what you've heard. You say you love God and want to change, but only if it's on your terms. I think the real issue here is pride."

Follow Scott's example. Stomp out pride.

• **Allow the Lord to destroy spiritual cancer—pride.** Even though "bad company corrupts good character" (1 Corinthians 15:33), the pride in the heart of the teen from Pennsylvania caused him to follow friends who'd rather slander God's name than honor it. Despite the fact that Jesus wants Christians to tune their minds (and ears) in to stuff that's "true, noble, right, pure, lovely, admirable, excellent, praiseworthy"(Philippians 4:8), his prideful side wouldn't stop feeding on music muck. Regardless of his responsibility to let the Word of Christ dwell in him (Colossians 3:16), his pride kept him resistant to the Bible.

• **Nurture the opposite of pride: humility, love, contentment, common sense.** As Scott from California discovered, the key to overcoming any sin in our lives—whether it's an issue with lust or a messed-up mouth—involves allowing the Lord to clean up our heart first. If we can face up to the pride in our lives, Jesus will build in us the spiritual muscle to resist anything else life dishes out.

• **PRAY IT OUT: "Lord, remove the pride from my heart."** Ask God to examine your heart. If pride is present, pray for divine surgery. Ask Him to remove this form of spiritual cancer.

TRIBAL MARKS

A KEY POINT I LEARNED TODAY:

_____

_____

_____

_____

_____

_____

HOW I WANT TO GROW:

_____

_____

_____

_____

_____

MY PRAYER LIST:

_____

_____

_____

_____

_____

_____

SURVIVOR SECRETS

▶▶▶**WEEKLY MEMORY VERSE**: *But you are a chosen people, a royal priesthood, a holy nation, a people belonging to God, that you may declare the praises of him who called you out of darkness into his wonderful light. Once you were not a people, but now you are the people of God; once you had not received mercy, but now you have received mercy.* —**1 Peter 2:9-10**

TRIBAL QUEST

Strive to be a Christian who is sturdy and reliable—an honorable young man who does what is right regardless of what's popular.

EXPLORE THE WORD: **Matthew 1:18-25**

TRIBAL TRUTH

"Joseph son of David, do not be afraid to take Mary home as your wife, because what is conceived in her is from the Holy Spirit. She will give birth to a son, and you are to give him the name Jesus, because he will save his people from their sins." —**Matthew 1:20-21**

TRIBAL FACE

Joseph of Nazareth—Redefining Honor

Despite not having much wealth, life is good for Joseph. He enjoys working with his hands—building, creating, shaping, pounding. His trade as a carpenter keeps him busy, and the future looks bright for this upstanding Nazarene. A smile stretches across his face as he smoothes the rough surface of a wooden door he has made. Once put into place on his neighbor's house, the oak barrier will be sturdy and reliable for years to come—much like Joseph himself.

Sturdy and reliable—a righteous man who keeps the law diligently. This is the kind of person Joseph was raised to be. After all, his family can trace their ancestry back to King David.

But Joseph has a new reason to live up to his family's proud heritage. He has given his heart to a beautiful young lady named Mary. (A big wedding ceremony is in the works.) Joseph imagines the countless memories Mary and he will share as husband and wife: hearty meals by a crackling fire, endless talks late into the night, the laughter of children—lots of children. Joseph dreams of filling his home with sons and daughters!

Then one day, his dreams are crushed.

"Mary. Oh, my beautiful Mary. What's wrong? You seem different somehow. Happy, almost glowing—yet frightened, as well."

His bride-to-be blinks away a tear and lowers her head, placing Joseph's hand on her abdomen. Mary looks up again and meets his shocked expression with an uneasy nod.

Yes. There is a baby in Mary's womb! But how—why?

Joseph pulls his hand back and quietly leaves. Distraught, he walks aimlessly through the village. He eventually comes to his house and steps inside. Joseph latches the door behind him, curls up on the floor, and begins to weep.

How could this happen? How could she betray me this way? There's only one thing to do: release her from marriage. She must wed the father of the child.

Strangely, though, Joseph feels no rage, only a great disappointment that settles like a permanent knot in his chest, weighing him down and making it hard to breathe. How could his judgment have been so flawed, so far from the mark? He had looked forward to marrying the young woman whose character and temperament had made her seem all the more likable.[2]

Joseph wipes the tears from his eyes and drifts off to sleep. Suddenly, the voice of an angel calls to him in a dream.

"Joseph, son of David," the angel says, "you should not fear to take Mary home as your wife, because the Infant conceived in her is of the Holy Spirit. She will bear a son, and when she does you must call His name Jesus, since He will save His people from their sins. God is fulfilling prophecies, Joseph!

"Behold, a virgin shall conceive and bear a son, and His name shall be called Emmanuel."

"Emmanuel," the angel says. "Emmanuel, God with us."[3]

Then Joseph wakes up and does exactly what God's angel commanded in the dream. He trusts the Lord, even if it defies common sense, even if it threatens all of his well-laid plans and hopes and dreams, even if it means ridicule and shame and being misunderstood by others. He knows that this is one special Child growing inside Mary.

So, he takes his bride home as his wife, but he does not consummate the marriage until she has the baby. Then he names the Child Jesus.

Mary's pregnancy put Joseph in a desperate position: How could he uphold his integrity and reputation when his fiancee had become pregnant?

He planned to divorce her quietly, which, in that culture, would have been gracious, sparing her and her family from terrible disgrace. From all Joseph knew at that point, Mary had committed adultery, and according to the law, the penalty was death for her and dishonor for her family (see Deuteronomy 22:13-21). To understand how offensive Mary's pregnancy was, we have to examine ancient Jewish culture.

The Jews had a special custom for couples getting married. Before they could marry, the couple would enter an engagement period called a betrothal, which would normally last about one year. After the waiting period, the couple married and only then joined together in sexual union.

But this betrothal differed significantly from modern engagements. Once a man and woman were betrothed, everyone considered them as good as married. Although they reserved sex for marriage (after the betrothal period), people already called them husband and wife. Only death or divorce could dissolve the bond. They couldn't get "cold feet" or date around to find a better mate: They had essentially tied the knot.

One of the purposes was to see whether the couple would remain faithful to each other. If the woman got pregnant by another man, thus breaking her vow to her husband, he could legally divorce her for her offense and make a public mockery of her for her sin.

Joseph discovered Mary's pregnancy. What would he do? His response shows his true character:

Joseph listened to God. He heard what God planned to do through Mary and the Child she bore. Yet to follow the instructions given, Joseph had to do more than just listen.

Joseph believed God. He could have laughed at God or blamed his strange vision on the previous night's matzo balls. But he believed. He didn't have to take Mary as his wife. He didn't have to call the Boy's name Jesus. But he had heard the message and believed it as true. How do we know he believed?

Joseph obeyed God. He did what God told him to do. The Scriptures purposely use the same language to describe both what God commanded and what Joseph did. What did God tell him to do? He said two things: "Take Mary home as your wife, because what is conceived in her is from the Holy Spirit. She will give birth to a son, and you are to give him the name Jesus" (Matthew 1:20-21). And what did Joseph do? When he arose from his sleep—he didn't put it off for weeks, but acted immediately—he "took Mary home as his wife" and when the Son was born, "he gave him the name Jesus" (Matthew 1:24-25).

The Bible tells us something else about Joseph's righteous character: He "kept [Mary] a virgin until she gave birth to a Son" (Matthew 1:25, NASB). Imagine getting married and waiting months before having sex with your wife! But Joseph placed preserving God's ways above fulfilling his own fleshly desires. There would be no question about the source of this Child—the Holy Spirit.

Joseph displayed his righteousness through listening, believing, and obeying God. Perhaps he experienced gossip from some, or ostracism from others, yet he did not compromise his integrity. His example set the standard for all who strive to be men of honor. Consider this observation from authors Ann Spangler and Robert Wolgemuth in their book, *Men of the Bible*: "During the formative years of the Messiah's childhood, Joseph lived a consistent and exemplary life of faithfulness and obedience to God. Imagine how important it was that Jesus grew up with a father whose character was worthy of emulating."[4]

Are you serious about cultivating the marks of a battle-ready warrior? Do you want to be an honorable young man who has a reputation for godliness? Set your eyes on the character of Joseph, one of the true unsung heroes of the Bible.[5]

TRIBAL TRAINING

• **Listen when God speaks.** When you have a close relationship with Jesus, He will direct your steps, telling you Himself how He wants you to handle a particular situation. He communicates with you throughout the day, answering your questions and guiding you. You literally walk in His presence minute by minute. Does God talk to people with an audible voice? Not usually. In fact, He rarely communicates with most of us this way, if ever. Instead, the Holy Spirit deals with each human being in a personal and intimate way, convicting, directing, and influencing us.

Think about those times when you faced a temptation of some sort. (Maybe it was lying . . . or lust.) Remember how that "something inside" seemed to kick in, telling you to turn away? More than likely, that "something" was the Holy Spirit, directing you to the will of God. Of course, the Lord gave you free will to follow Him—or to disobey.

It's a good idea to get in the habit of asking yourself these questions daily: What is God saying to me today? What has God already told me that I know I need to obey? Pray without ceasing? Keep my body pure?

- **Believe God's Word.** Despite what some people say, the Bible is more relevant than ever. It teaches us how to live in purity with a girlfriend, stay out of debt, keep sweeping even when the boss is out of the room, and keep going after getting cut from the basketball team. Most importantly, Scripture teaches us how to grow closer to God. But for it to affect us, we have to believe it. We believe it because we believe its Author. We must believe God as Joseph believed God.

- **Obey God—even when nobody's looking.** The Lord keeps you in His sight, and He looks favorably on those who walk with integrity. If we want genuine faith, we need to follow Joseph's example and put our faith into action—obeying the Lord in public, as well as when we're alone.

"At times, God will be the only witness to your righteous behavior," says popular author Henry T. Blackaby. "The most important thing is not that people know the truth. The most important thing is that you are a person of integrity before God"[6]

So, if the Lord tells you something through His Word, such as to "flee from youthful lusts" (2 Timothy 2:22, NASB), do you claim to obey in public, then make excuses in private? We often struggle to obey God, but active obedience confirms true faith.

- **PRAY IT OUT: "Lord, help me to be a man of honor like Joseph."** Ask God to enable you to honor Him with your words, your actions, and your life.

TRIBAL MARKS

A KEY POINT I LEARNED TODAY:

_____

_____

_____

_____

_____

_____

HOW I WANT TO GROW:

_____

_____

_____

_____

_____

_____

MY PRAYER LIST:

_____

_____

_____

_____

_____

_____

_____

SURVIVOR SECRETS

▶▶▶**WEEKLY MEMORY VERSE**: *But you are a chosen people, a royal priesthood, a holy nation, a people belonging to God, that you may declare the praises of him who called you out of darkness into his wonderful light. Once you were not a people, but now you are the people of God; once you had not received mercy, but now you have received mercy.* —**1 Peter 2:9-10**

TRIBAL QUEST

Don't get lost in a crowd of sinners. In the face of sneers, jeers, and rolling eyes, determine to be a man of God.

EXPLORE THE WORD: **Genesis 6-9**

TRIBAL TRUTH

The LORD *then said to Noah, "Go into the ark, you and your whole family, because I have found you righteous in this generation."* —**Genesis 7:1**

TRIBAL FACE

Noah

Following God, Not Man

Destroyed? Every living, breathing thing on the face of the earth wiped away—as if none of it had ever been created?

The possibility is almost too much to bear. Yet judgment is at hand. The unthinkable will happen, just as God had said:

"The LORD saw how great man's wickedness on the earth had become, and that every inclination of the thoughts of his heart was only evil all the time.

The LORD was grieved that he had made man on the earth, and his heart was filled with pain.

So the LORD said, 'I will wipe mankind, whom I have created, from the face of the earth—men and animals, and creatures that move along the ground, and birds of the air—for I am grieved that I have made them.'"[7]

But Noah found favor in the eyes of the Lord. The man God describes as "righteous, blameless among the people of his time" has been spared. He and his family have been set apart by the Creator for an important purpose.

Noah peers out the door of the ark he had built and shudders. The clouds are dark and eerie. The air smells like death. Then he catches some angry stares from his neighbors. *Why won't they listen?* he wonders. *Why are they so stubborn, so foolish? And why do they insist that I'm the foolish one?*

Not one person in all the land other than Noah and his family will follow God. Instead, they worship idols and pursue their own sinful pleasures. They ridicule the thought of being faithful to God and mock Noah for his obedience.

"Look at the crazy old man. He's built himself a boat in the middle of nowhere!"

"Insane, I tell you. He claims it's going to flood. 'Repent,' he says, 'or be destroyed.' Noah's the one who is already destroyed—destroyed in the mind, that is!"

Despite being unpopular and vastly outnumbered, Noah refused to waver. He spent one hundred years erecting an ark out of reverence to God.

Noah's mind replays the Lord's detailed instructions:

"'Build yourself a ship from teakwood. Make rooms in it. Coat it with pitch inside and out. Make it 450 feet long, seventy-five feet wide, and forty-five feet high. Build a roof for it and put in a window eighteen inches from the top; put in a door on the side of the ship; and make three decks; lower, middle and upper.

"'I'm going to bring a flood on the Earth that will destroy everything alive under Heaven. Total destruction.

"'But I'm going to establish a covenant with you: You'll board the ship, and your sons, your wife and your sons' wives will come on board with you. You are also to take two of each living creature, a male and a female, on board the ship, to preserve their lives with you: two of every species of bird, mammal, and reptile—two of everything so as to preserve their lives along with yours. Also get all the food you'll need and store it up for you and them.'"[8]

Noah had done everything just as God commanded him.

The faithful servant takes one last look outside, then steps into the ark with his family. It is time.

God shuts the door behind Noah, and the rain begins to fall.

It's as dark of an account as there is in the Bible. So reprehensible were people's lives, God reaches terrible despair for creating the human race. So, He decides to send a great flood that will destroy them, all except for one man and his family.

The story of Noah is the story about us, of course. It tells a timeless truth: If left to ourselves as a race, we are doomed. It also tells the truth about judgment, about God's anger—a threat bigger than people can imagine, a judgment closer than most of us think.[9]

Despite living in what was perhaps history's most wicked age, Noah stood out of the crowd. In the face of sneers, jeers, and rolling eyes, he wasn't afraid to resist "blending in." Instead, Noah clung to what was right—even when *right* wasn't popular. He chose to walk with God, not follow in the footsteps of his peers. He persevered under pressure.

Noah's life was so exemplary that in the middle of all the debauchery, he found favor in God's eyes. Noah was righteous and blameless among the people of his time. Because of his faithfulness, he was the one man whom the Lord chose not to destroy.[10]

When it comes to your own life, do you feel like the only young man in youth group who's serious about following Christ? Does it seem as if you're the last virgin on campus? Are you beginning to wonder if the battle to stay sexually pure is really worth it? You, too, can find assurance from Noah's example. Like the culture he lived in, the one that surrounds us today is drowning in immorality. And like Noah, you can choose to persevere under pressure and stand firm in obedience to God. The tricky part comes with trying to figure out what submission to God looks like. How do we live it out practically in our daily lives? And what should we expect as the result of this level of radical obedience?

Keep reading. (The next few paragraphs offer a few clues.)

TRIBAL TRAINING

• **Choose to walk with the Lord.** It was the secret to Noah's success. For him, surrender was not a single decision that resulted from a mountaintop experience; it was a daily process, a journey, a walk. Walking with God meant knowing him. Knowing God meant loving him. Loving meant hearing. Hearing, obeying.[11]

• **Rely on the "principles etched in your soul."** It has been said that you can learn the history of the entire twentieth century by reading the biographies of seven men: Vladimir Lenin, Joseph Stalin, Adolf Hitler, Mao Tse-tung, Theodore Roosevelt, Winston Churchill, and Ronald Reagan. While only three of these men were heroes (you can guess which ones), each had the capacity to stand strong under pressure. And one leader in particular, Reagan, daily turned to

God for strength and guidance when the path ahead seemed unclear. Here's what President George W. Bush had to say about America's 40th commander in chief: "He [Ronald Reagan] knew that a true leader sets clear goals and makes decisions based upon principles etched in his soul."[12]

• **Strive to be an overcomer.** When temptation hits and you feel like giving in, ask yourself this question: What's holding me back from obeying God? Fear? Peer pressure? A shortage in the "motivation department"? Then tell yourself . . .

> *I CAN overcome temptation and resist sin because the Holy Spirit has empowered me to do so.* **Tribal Truth:** *1 Corinthians 10:13.*

> *I CAN overcome my past mistakes because Jesus Christ broke the chains and set me free to live in wholeness, in fullness— completely forgiving my sin and cleansing my soul.* **Tribal Truth:** *2 Peter 1:4-9.*

> *I CAN overcome the world and live in obedience to God because He is renewing my mind and directing my steps.* **Tribal Truth:** *Romans 12:2.*

• **Know the rewards of joining Noah's "Overcomer Club."** Those who overcome the world and strive to live uprightly for God can expect great rewards. Here's what the book of Revelation says:

Revelation 2:7—"To him who overcomes, I will give the right to eat from the tree of life, which is in the paradise of God."

Revelation 2:11—"He who overcomes will not be hurt at all by the second death."

Revelation 2:17—"To him who overcomes, I will give some of the hidden manna. I will also give him a white stone with a new name written on it, known only to him who receives it."

Revelation 2:26-28—"To him who overcomes and does my will to the end, I will give authority over the nations—'He will rule them with an iron scepter; he will dash them to pieces like pottery'—just as I have received authority from my Father. I will also give him the morning star."

Revelation 3:5—"He who overcomes will, like them, be dressed in white. I will never blot out his name from the book of life, but will acknowledge his name before my Father and his angels."

Revelation 3:12—"Him who overcomes I will make a pillar in the temple of my God. Never again will he leave it. I will write on him the name of my God and the name of the city of my God, the new Jerusalem, which is coming down out of heaven from my God; and I will also write on him my new name."

Revelation 3:21—"To him who overcomes, I will give the right to sit with me on my throne, just as I overcame and sat down with my Father on his throne."

Revelation 21:7—"He who overcomes will inherit all this, and I will be his God and he will be my son."

• **PRAY IT OUT: "Lord, give me the strength to persevere under pressure."** Ask Jesus to help you overcome temptation and sin. Ask Him to seek you out of the crowd.

▶▶▶ CONSIDER LIVING OUT THIS LESSON FROM
HENRY T. BLACKABY:

> *Noah was not lost to God in the crowd of sinners. God noticed every act of Noah's righteousness. Noah had chosen to live uprightly before God despite what everyone around him was doing, and God had observed him. There may have been times when Noah wondered if it mattered if he lived a righteous life, since no one else was. Yet he continued, and his persistence in righteousness saved his life and the lives of his family members.*[13]

TRIBAL MARKS

A KEY POINT I LEARNED TODAY:

_____

_____

_____

_____

_____

_____

HOW I WANT TO GROW:

_____

_____

_____

_____

_____

_____

MY PRAYER LIST:

_____

_____

_____

_____

_____

_____

_____

DAY 27: HE CHOOSES TO BE A CHRIST-BUILT WARRIOR

▶▶▶**WEEKLY MEMORY VERSE**: *But you are a chosen people, a royal priesthood, a holy nation, a people belonging to God, that you may declare the praises of him who called you out of darkness into his wonderful light. Once you were not a people, but now you are the people of God; once you had not received mercy, but now you have received mercy.* —**1 Peter 2:9-10**

TRIBAL QUEST

Strive to fit your desires and goals into God's will for your life, allowing Him to mold you into the Christ-built warrior He created you to be.

EXPLORE THE WORD: **Philippians 3:12-21**

TRIBAL TRUTH

Brothers, I do not consider myself yet to have taken hold of it. But one thing I do: Forgetting what is behind and straining toward what is ahead, I press on toward the goal to win the prize for which God has called me heavenward in Christ Jesus. —**Philippians 3:13-14**

TRIBAL FACE

Jeremy, 22
Colorado Springs, Colorado
Seeking a Prize Greater than Gold

Faster! The coach's words scream through Jeremy's head. *Faster on each turn! Seventy laps! No rest!*

He and the five other speed skaters look like a long train as they race around the 400-meter ice rink. Jeremy is tailing the lead skater for now, but on the next turn, he'll pull off and drop to the rear of the pack. Then it's Jeremy's turn to pace as hard as he can, with the other guys following him.

Every muscle is surging with pain, and his heart is pounding so hard, it hurts to breathe. *How'd I ever get nicknames like "Colorado Flash" or "Jean-Claude Van Jeremy"?*

"GO! GO! GO!" barks the coach, as Jeremy takes the lead.

He shrugs off the stinging razors tearing through his quadriceps and focuses on his goal: competing in the Winter Olympic Games.

Building endurance and pushing his 22-year-old body to its limit six to eight hours a day, six days a week, is the only way to get there. "But if I didn't believe it was God's will for my life," he tells the other racers, "I wouldn't spend another second on the ice."

As this book goes to press, Jeremy still hasn't made it to the Olympics. But he hasn't put away his skates. "Speed skating in the Olympics is my dream," he says, "yet if I don't make it, I'll put it in the past and look forward to whatever else God has planned for me. I know that everything that happens to me is for a purpose. God's purpose. And His purpose is always best."

Jeremy has anchored his life to the right goal: He is striving to be a Christ-built warrior (a young man who seeks God's will and God's ways). And the discipline and commitment are paying off. Each day, his body grows stronger, his skills sharpen, and he's one step closer to fulfilling his dreams. His faith in God is deepening, too. The more this athlete spends training his spiritual life—reading the Bible, praying, and seeking His guidance—the more God reveals Himself to Jeremy.

The fact is, God's will is revealed when we seek Him. God has already mapped out our lives since birth. But it's entirely up to Him when He decides to make His presence and power known directly to us. And once this happens, our lives are forever changed.

TRIBAL TRAINING

• **Steer clear of distractions.** Especially the ones that'll take you down a nowhere track. You know—a lust for money (instead of God's riches), an appetite for immoral sex (instead of the genuine love that Christ offers), a thirst for alcohol or drugs (instead of the joy of pleasing your Creator).

• **Get on an eternal track.** Just as an athlete gives his or her all to a sport, Christians need to give the same commitment to God. Once you put God first in your life and trust Him with all your heart, He will show you His power—power that you never imagined. His will for you far surpasses any of your own dreams and goals.

• **Keep your balance.** Satan knows exactly the right buttons to push! He sees your weak points and goes after them. But he can't destroy you; that is, if you don't let him. No matter how bad life gets, no matter how much you sin, Jesus still loves you. But it hurts the Lord when you disobey Him. Christ wept for your sin, and He yearns for you to come back to Him. When you blow it, confess your sin to God and ask Him to help you get your life on the right track again.

• **PRAY IT OUT: "Lord, mold me into a Christ-built warrior—the kind of man You created me to be."** Ask God to help you seek His will and His purpose for your life.

A KEY POINT I LEARNED TODAY:

_____

_____

_____

_____

_____

_____

HOW I WANT TO GROW:

_____

_____

_____

_____

_____

_____

MY PRAYER LIST:

_____

_____

_____

_____

_____

_____

SURVIVOR SECRETS

▶▶▶**WEEKLY MEMORY VERSE**: *But you are a chosen people, a royal priesthood, a holy nation, a people belonging to God, that you may declare the praises of him who called you out of darkness into his wonderful light. Once you were not a people, but now you are the people of God; once you had not received mercy, but now you have received mercy.* —**1 Peter 2:9-10**

TRIBAL QUEST

Sexual purity is not the final goal. Seeing Jesus face to face is. When that day comes, you want to hear the words "Well done."

EXPLORE THE WORD: Acts 6:1-7

TRIBAL TRUTH

"His master replied, 'Well done, good and faithful servant! You have been faithful with a few things; I will put you in charge of many things. Come and share your master's happiness!'" —**Matthew 25:21**

TRIBAL FACE

Stephen

Deacon to the Needy

Stephen had a simple, humble job: distribute donations from the food bank to poor Christian widows. In other words, he was a waiter in a restaurant where they gave no tips. They called him a "deacon." It was a ministry he took seriously, a trust he carried out to the fullest.

But on the side, in his "spare time," he did miracles. Wondrous, awesome miracles. The kind of things God used to show people that Jesus was still alive and real. Stephen's miracles came packaged with convincing arguments that Jesus, the Righteous One, was exactly who He said He was, the Son of God and Sin-Bearer for the world.

It doesn't seem like Stephen was married. No girlfriend, either. He was too busy serving Jesus. No time for a woman.

In contrast, his fellow waiter/deacon, Philip, *was* married; he had four daughters to raise (Acts 21:9). And Philip was just as busy as Stephen, serving God all over the place during his "spare time." His most famous assignment was chasing the chariot of some Ethiopian rich guy to tell him about the Jesus of Isaiah 53.

So, it's not about being a bachelor or being a married guy. It's about serving Jesus with all your heart.

And Stephen did so. To the death. A death so brave, so forgiving, so heavenly minded, that the man who ordered it, Saul, would have his conscience seriously bothered from that day forward. In dying, Stephen helped Saul see the Light.

The interesting thing about Stephen's last moments on earth is that he saw Jesus *standing* at the right hand of God. Jesus normally *sits* at the right hand of God. But with Stephen about to exit Earth and head for Heaven, Jesus stood in smiling anticipation of His faithful servant's arrival.

Is the possibility that Jesus will be standing when you arrive, arms open wide, something that excites you?

It should.

The more you think about that day in heaven, the purer your today on Earth will be. John, whose own blood brother was also murdered for serving Jesus, put it this way: "We shall be like him, for we shall see him as he is. Everyone who has this hope in him purifies himself, just as he is pure" (1 John 3:2-3). Guys who think only about today are hugely prone to temptation, because selfish sex is about here, now, and who cares about tomorrow? But you have a different perspective, right? A long-range perspective.

You're living today with eternity in mind.

Years later, Stephen's executioner would pen these words: "I press on to take hold of that for which Christ Jesus took hold of me. Brothers, I do not consider myself yet to have taken hold of it. But one thing I do: Forgetting what is behind and straining toward what is ahead, I press on toward the goal to win the prize for which God has called me heavenward in Christ Jesus" (Philippians 3:12-14). Paul's sense of calling echoed deeply in the chambers of his soul. He knew his existence was not about having fun, earning money, being successful, or playing basketball with the Orlando Magic. His goal was something far greater.

What's the goal? Jesus—His Person, His character, His Spirit—shining through your life. Elsewhere, Paul put it this way: "And we, who with unveiled faces all reflect the Lord's glory, are being transformed into his likeness with ever-increasing glory" (2 Corinthians 3:18). A total, daily, glorious, growing transformation. Jesus' likeness. That's your goal.

What's the prize? It's so huge, it's multi-faceted: gold, silver, precious stones—for starters. Eternal crowns to lay at Christ's feet. For those who can endure the suffering that serving Jesus involves, an opportunity to reign side by side with Him in His future kingdom (see 2 Timothy 2:12). And for those motivated by simple appreciation, the words, "Well done, good and faithful servant." To hear that from Jesus is worth dying for.

It's worth living for, too.

I once read about a missionary to a remote group of tribal Indians in South America. He spent years loving the people, learning their language, serving them in any way he could. His greatest desire, of course, was to tell them about Jesus.

No one wanted to listen.

When drought hit the area, the missionary found himself without the means to eat. The little food available was hoarded by the people he had come to reach for Jesus. This nameless missionary slowly starved to death, praying God would find a way to save those who were too stingy to keep him alive. After his death, the consciences of these tribal Indians were seriously bothered. Many eventually saw the Light.

In the meantime, that missionary has heard the words, "Well done."

Words worth living and dying for.

TRIBAL TRAINING

• **Strive to know your calling, your vision, your direction in life.** Have you unconsciously accepted the world's oh-so-pitifully-shortsighted goal of getting a good job, finding a pretty wife, owning a nice house, raising 2.3 kids, retiring near a golf course, and dying with an expensive grave marker? None of those things, in and of themselves, is wrong. But if they're your ultimate goal, you're totally wrong. You need to take a hard look at what's really motivating you.

• **Accept the truth.** As a follower of Jesus Christ, you have a higher calling: You're to serve Him with all your heart. And in the process of serving Him, you'll let God transform your soul into the likeness of Jesus. That's your calling. That needs to be your bottom-line goal. If it is, you'll be evaluating your motives, setting good objectives, and taking real action to make that big objective happen. You are called by God to a high calling: living like Jesus and serving Jesus. No doubts there. The question is: Are you listening? Have you truly heard the call?

• **PRAY IT OUT: "Lord, allow me to hear and accept Your call on my life."** Ask Jesus to give you the courage to "live" Him and to serve Him.

TRIBAL MARKS

A KEY POINT I LEARNED TODAY:

_____

_____

_____

_____

_____

_____

HOW I WANT TO GROW:

_____

_____

_____

_____

_____

_____

MY PRAYER LIST:

_____

_____

_____

_____

_____

_____

_____

NOTES

Introduction

1. Henry T. Blackaby and Richard Blackaby, *Experiencing God Day-By-Day: A Devotional* (Nashville: Broadman & Holman Publishers, 1998), 328.

Week 1

1. Henry T. Blackaby and Richard Blackaby, *Experiencing God Day-By-Day: A Devotional* (Nashville: Broadman & Holman Publishers, 1998), 242.

Week 2

1. Information gleaned from an interview with Joann Cordie, licensed counselor and sex-addiction specialist.
2. Justin Lookadoo, *The Dirt on Sex* (Grand Rapids, Mich.: Revell, 2004), 8.
3. Adapted from "The Art of Nondating" by Greg Trine with Michael Ross, *Breakaway magazine*, February 1996, 27.

Week 3

1. Kurt Bruner and Jim Ware, *Finding God in the Lord of the Rings* (Carol Stream, Ill.: Tyndale House Publishers, 2001), 66.
2. Patrick A. Means, *Men's Secret Wars* (Grand Rapids, Mich.: Revell, 1999), 176.
3. Ibid., 177–178.
4. Ibid., 225–226.
5. Robert S. McGee, *The Search for Significance*, Student Edition (Nashville: W Publishing Group, 2003), 105.
6. Peter Marshall, *Mr. Jones, Meet the Master* (New York: Revell, 1949), 177–178.
7. Max Lucado, *He Still Moves Stones* (Nashville: Word, 1993), 110.
8. Ibid.
9. Dorothy M. Stewart, *The Westminster Collection of Christian Prayers* (Louisville, Ky.: John Knox Press, 2002), 49.
10. Oswald Chambers, *My Utmost for His Highest* (New York: Dodd, Mead, & Company, 1935), January 15.
11. Charles H. Spurgeon, quoted in Calvin Miller, *The Book of Jesus* (New York: Simon & Schuster, 1996), 51–52.

Week 4

1. C.S. Lewis, *Mere Christianity* (New York: HarperCollins, 2001), 121–122.
2. Ann Spangler and Robert Wolgemuth, *Men of the Bible* (Grand Rapids, Mich.: Zondervan, 2002), 318–319.
3. Walter Wangerin Jr., *The Book of God* (Grand Rapids, Mich.: Zondervan, 1996), 588.
4. Spangler and Wolgemuth, 323.
5. A portion of this devotional lesson was adapted from "Father of Jesus," *Breakaway* magazine, December 2004, 27–28.
6. Blackaby and Blackaby, *Experiencing God Day-By-Day*, 184
7. See Genesis 6:5–7.
8. Eugene H. Peterson, *The Message Remix* (Colorado Springs: Navpress, 2003), 44.
9. Dirk R. Buursma and Verlyn D. Verbugge, *Daylight Devotional Bible* (Grand Rapids, Mich.: Zondervan, 1988), 9.
10. Spangler and Wolgemuth, 35.
11. Ibid.
12. Cited from *Fox News Report*, June 8, 2004.
13. Blackaby and Blackaby, E*xperiencing God Day-by-Day*, 166.

FOCUS ON THE FAMILY®

teen outreach

At Focus on the Family, we work to help you really get to know Jesus and equip you to change your world for Him.

We realize the struggles you face are different from your parents' or your little brother's, so we've developed a lot of resources specifically to help you live boldly for Christ, no matter what's happening in your life.

Besides teen events and a live call-in show, we have Web sites, magazines, booklets, devotionals and novels ... all dealing with the stuff you care about. For a detailed listing of the latest resources, log on to our Web site at **go.family.org/teens.**

***Breakaway*®**
Teen guys
breakawaymag.com

***Brio*®**
Teen girls 13 to 15
briomag.com

Focus on the Family Magazines

We know you want to stay up-to-date on the latest in your world — but it's hard to find information on relationships, entertainment, trends and teen issues that doesn't drag you down. It's even harder to find magazines that deliver what you want and need from a Christ-honoring perspective.

That's why we created *Breakaway* (for teen guys), *Brio* (for teen girls 12 to 16), *Brio & Beyond* (for girls ages 16 and up). So, don't be left out — sign up today!

***Brio & Beyond*®**
Teen girls 16 to 19
briomag.com

 Phone toll free: (800) A-FAMILY (232-6459)
In Canada, call toll free: (800) 661-9800

BP06XTN

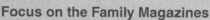